C000178602

NELLIE'S
A Life of S

This book is written by Elizabeth Ellen Osborne, aged 85 and grandchild of Michael Thomas Scott. It is dedicated to her father and mother, Mr and Mrs Charles Jones Whalley, her sister Mrs Joyce Hough and her own family – husband Ralph, daughters Veronica and Diana, and their families.

December 1999

ELIZABETH ELLEN OSBORNE

NELLIE'S STORY
A LIFE OF SERVICE

an imprint of
ANNE LOADER
PUBLICATIONS

I never thought that this story would go beyond my family's bookcases and I say 'thank you' to Mrs Anne Loader and her husband Jack for their hard work and the interest they have taken in spreading my story further afield.
Elizabeth E Osborne
('Nellie')

ISBN 1 901253 15 5

First published April 2000

Edited, typeset and published in Gt Britain by:
Léonie Press
an imprint of
Anne Loader Publications
13 Vale Road
Hartford
Northwich
Cheshire CW8 1PL

Printed by:
Anne Loader Publications

Contents

List of Illustrations

Many thanks to Mrs Betty Worrall for the loan of several photographs of Davenham in times past

CHAPTER ONE

Early Days

My carers, Mr and Mrs Robinson

*I*n 1850 a baby boy was born in Castlebar County Mayo, Ireland. He had three sisters. One emigrated to America, one went to County Cork and Nora stayed in Castlebar. She was the only one to keep in touch with her family over the years.

The boy, my grandfather, was christened Michael Thomas Scott. At the age of twelve he ran away from home, made his way over to England and eventually arrived in Cheshire.

He must have been a very determined boy, for he got work on farms and became very well known years later as a highly skilled hedger and ditcher. When he layered a hedge it was a work of art. As a child I saw one of his ditches: it was so clean and the sides were so smooth, with the clear water

1

running happily on its way to the River Dane. This boy grew up in Cheshire and as far as I can gather he got married in the early 1880s.

He and his wife had two children, a boy named Thomas and a girl called Elizabeth – my mother. I believe they lived in Moulton and I was told that the only memory Elizabeth had of her mother was seeing her 'in a box'. That, of course, was her coffin, for she died when Elizabeth was about three years old. None of her mother's family came to see what was happening to those children, they were just left to the mercy of the world. Their father disappeared for some reason, so the welfare authorities took them to Northwich Workhouse, which was the equivalent of going into today's 'council care', and – apart from the street – the only place for homeless children.

I learned later that Elizabeth and Tom had a life of misery during the years they spent there.

When she was old enough Elizabeth went to Timber Lane School, in Northwich. It was demolished years ago.

I am not sure how old they were when Mrs Ann Latham took them to live with her at Moulton. A girl named Millie also lived there, but we have no information about her. I only know that she and Elizabeth were so alike that we now wonder if they were related in some way. They were very close until Millie died. I still thank Ann in my heart for her kindness.

Life was very hard for families then and the main source of work was in the salt mines at Meadow Bank, Winsford. I believe it was a common thing to see children on what they called the cinder banks, filling bags and trucks with cinders from the boilers and taking them home for fuel. That was a job to do before they had any breakfast, then they went to school.

Between 11.40am and 11.45am the children were let out to go to the salt works with their fathers' dinner contained in a basin, wrapped up in a red handkerchief. I knew of this

2

when I was young because it still went on then. Elizabeth and Tom were both what they called 'cinder collectors'.

When Elizabeth left school in 1900 she went to work as a servant girl at Thorn Farm, Chester Road, Hartford, the home of Mr and Mrs Arthur Stubbs. They were very hard taskmasters and I've heard all about the long hours and hard work she put in. The Stubbs had three daughters, Annie, Lily and Bessie. Annie was Elizabeth's age, and they became quite friendly. I believe this helped her to bear a lot of the bad times she had in front of her.

She was called 'Lizzie' when she started to work at Thorn Farm and it stuck with her all her life.

One evening she put on a nice blouse because she was going to wait on table for a dinner party and wanted to look tidy. Mrs Stubbs on seeing it said: "Get up those stairs and put something on to suit your station. People will think you are one of the guests."

The blouse only had a bit of lace round the collar. My mother told me of this and many more incidents.

When she was about eighteen years old she began to have

Thorn Farm, Chester Road, Hartford (now demolished)

3

a lot of pain in her face and something like an abscess appeared on
her cheekbone. Her doctor discovered something was very wrong
and she went into the Victoria
Infirmary in Northwich for an
operation. She was told that if a
piece of bone were removed she
would get better. This was not the
case. Over the next six years the
poor girl had five more operations
and the bridge of her nose was all
removed. Her sense of smell also
disappeared.

The last three times she was
unable to take the anaesthetic
because of the gap in her nose left
by the removal of the bone. I
understand that during the operations she could feel and hear the
surgeon's scalpel chipping and
scraping and she went through
hell. There weren't any effective
drugs in those days and part of the

My mother, Elizabeth (Lizzie)
Whalley

treatment was to have leeches put on her body to suck the
blood. It was called 'blood letting' and was supposed to heal.

There was very little sympathy at Thorn Farm. Lizzie had
to see that everything was in order and cleaned before she
went to the hospital, and she had to start working as soon
as she came back.

During the time she worked there she lost her brother
Tom. He was kicked by a horse and died as a result of his
injuries. This was a big blow to Lizzie because they were so
close. As far as I know she still had no idea where her father
was, so that left Mrs Latham and Millie as a substitute family. They were wonderful and Lizzie spent what little time

she had off with them 'at home', as she called it, in Moulton. She had some lovely kind friends – Sally Allcock, the Whalley families, Lizzie, Mary, Annie, Bob, Ernie, Charlie, George and Harriet. As time went on fate took a big part in their lives. Ernie fell in love with Lizzie and Sally fell in love with Charlie. After a few years the tables turned and Ernie married Sally Allcock and Lizzie married Charlie. The two couples were bosom friends all their lives.

Charlie was working at Shipbrook Hill Farm for Mr and Mrs Tom Parry. He applied for the tied cottage that went to the head man but he had to be married to be eligible for it, so he and Lizzie got married at Davenham church in 1912. They set up home at Shipbrook Cottages, Shipbrook and Lizzie – who had gone to work at Parry's some months before – carried on helping in the house. She also had the job of cleaning all the milk cans and tankards which were used to transport the milk to Manchester by train, daily. She also had to share the task of milking the cows, starting at 6am as the milk tankards had to be on the early train from Billinge

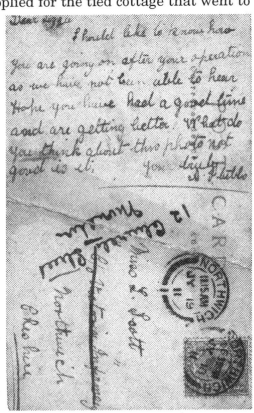

Postcard from Annie Stubbs to Lizzie after one of her painful operations; the reverse is the picture of Thorn Farm shown on page 3

5

Green platform.

The train was called the 'Dodger' and it travelled back and to between Sandbach and Northwich all day – the first stop at Billinge Green was at 7am in the town direction and the last stop there in the Northwich to Sandbach direction was at 10pm. The fare was 3d return, 2d single. This line closed to passengers about 1967-8 and the platform at Billinge was removed. By this time road transport had long been used to take the milk to Manchester. A family called Sant did this job for many years.

There were four tied farm cottages at Shipbrook, two lots of semis occupied by the Whalleys, Goughs, Athertons, and Robinsons, Eyre's small holding and Carter's Farm by the railway bridge. These were the close neighbours, the other farms were scattered quite a way off. All had families bar Charlie and Lizzie, and both Lizzie and Mrs Carter by the bridge were expecting babies in April. Their neighbour Mrs Robinson used to act as a midwife until the district nurse arrived. Believe it or not, she got a message from both women simultaneously to say that her services were needed. Anyway, she ended up going to the farm and Nurse Moore arrived at the cottage. Both babies were born within ten minutes of each other and on Mrs Eyre's birthday, April 2, 1914. I believe there were great celebrations.

Yes, you might have guessed, I was the cottage baby, christened 'Elizabeth Ellen', and the farm baby was called 'Elsie'. We grew up and remained very close friends until Elsie sadly passed away in 1993.

My very first memory is very vague. I am very small, I am walking slowly held by the hands by a man and woman. I have a white frock with a yoke and some sort of pinny on, and I'm on a cobbled path.

The next two recollections are very clear. I am with Patty Atherton. We are running up the road dragging my little sister Joyce along. There are buzzers blowing and church bells ringing, but we don't know why. I later learned it was to let everyone know that the 1914-18 war was over.

The other memory lasts longer. It concerns the world-wide epidemic of the Spanish influenza. I see my mother and sister in bed in the living room, with bottles of what I now know was medicine. I remember climbing on the chair, then on to the table and taking drinks from those bottles. I never got the 'flu. I also see a lady giving us all a drink of some thickish liquid, which I believe was gruel made with oatmeal.

This lady turned out to be Mrs Sandars, the rector's wife. The rector would be pacing up and down on the road outside the house while we were being fed. This happened twice a day and Mrs Stubbs from the farm down Manor Lane also helped with feeding the cottagers. Everyone seemed to be ill. I don't remember seeing my dad during this time, I believe he was running the farm single-handed.

I was told all about it when I was old enough to understand; apparently lots of people died of that terrible 'flu.

I must tell you about the houses and living conditions we had in those days. Our house was lovely. The front door opened on to a small square entrance hall with a nice clothes stand which held umbrellas and walking sticks. There was a small shelf with a mirror over it and up the sides were brass coat hooks, or 'pegs' as we called them.

This square lobby opened on to the front kitchen, and the stairs door led upstairs from this room. There was also the space under the stairs used for the coal store. The oven, and the hob on the side which held a big kettle full of water ready to be boiled, were both heated by coal fires. We also had a Dutch oven made of tin, very much like today's swing back lid type bread bin. It had a bar across the inside on which the bacon was hung and the eggs were cooked in the pan-like bottom, so that the hot bacon fat would drip on them. This little oven was attached to a bar in front of the coal fire to cook. How tasty this food was!

A door led to the back kitchen which also had a fireplace and oven just a shade smaller than the other one. There was also held a built-in boiler, heated by coal in the fireplace underneath, which was used on washing days. You can imagine the time it took to get the water to boiling point. To make it worse, all the drinking water and – if we got little rain – the bathing, washing and cleaning water had to be fetched from the pump in the Eyres' garden. We all took our buckets to get that from a very early age. Water was precious. I've known the time when we had to go to the back of Whatcroft Bluebell Wood to get water when everything was frozen up, and the spring down Parry's Cow Lane was the only available source. I am still very conscious to this day how I use water.

Off the back kitchen a door led to a lovely big pantry, with shelves round it.

All the floors had dark blue and red tiles, and our 'carpets' were pegged rag rugs in front of the fire. Making these was a winter night pastime, and they were beautiful. I could not believe my eyes when I saw the price of them at a shopping centre I went to recently!

Upstairs there were two bedrooms. The front one would hold four double beds and the back room two double beds, besides your other stuff.

There was no bathroom. The long tin bath hung on the wall outside, and was brought in at weekends for our weekly dip. The toilet was at the bottom of the very large garden. This was a properly built affair, with a tiled floor like the house and a slate roof. It held a contraption made of wood with a round hole. There was room for two more to sit and wait for you. The pan underneath was all boxed in at the front, and a door opened in the wall outside to allow the huge container to be taken out and emptied. This was done every week and the contents were buried in the garden.

We used paraffin oil lamps for lighting, and now and again candles. When we were small we had a nightlight on dark nights or very late when we paid our last visit to the toilet, often called the 'petty' in those days. We would use what we called a 'shippon lamp' – its real name was 'storm lamp'. We went down to the 'petty' in all weathers, that made no difference at all.

We were very lucky really because our coalmen were Hind and Swindells, and they delivered weekly. I remember at one time coal was 2/6d a bag. Paraffin, pots and pans, Jerry's Vim, Puritan soap, washing soda and all those sorts of goods were hawked by Mrs Buckley who had a covered horse drawn wagon. She rolled up every Friday night after a long day of going around all the farms in the district. She went far afield. There were always two or three children with her, and my memory is of a baby strapped to her body with a huge black shawl. One of those babies came to be our district nurse when she grew up, and she delivered many of Davenham's babies. Nurse Peggy Buckley was her name. She was loved by all.

The other lady who came round was Mrs Judy Lynch, who had a flat cart pulled by a mule. She collected rags and rabbit skins, and for those we received either 9d or rubbing stones to whiten the doorsteps. This was a ritual. I believe that was the beginning of Lynch's haulage firm. Bread was delivered by Mr Platt.

My mother always saw that the traders had a good hot drink and refreshments of sorts. She never failed them: it was always an open door. I remember one Good Friday, we were just going to sit down when a knock came on the front door. It was a man who asked for water, telling mother he was on a walk. With no more 'to do' he was invited to sit down with us for a meal. I can see the big oval dish with what must have been a huge piece of steamed cod on it, and there was lots of parsley sauce to go with it. He thanked Mum very much and said she would be hearing from him, but she never did.

I started school when I was five and walked the one and a half miles to Davenham. The older girls, Eva Robinson and Lizzie Atherton, took care of me and Patty, who had started six months previously. My first teacher was Miss Hewitt. She was quite elderly and sat in a bath chair all the time.

After a while Miss Hewitt left and Mrs Rose took her place. She was much younger and brought her own small daughter to school. Often when we arrived wet and cold after our long walk, hot cocoa was made for us and our coats and socks were hung to dry on the huge iron fire guard around a big coal fire. The caretaker whom we called 'Granny Atkins' carried the coal buckets to the classrooms and these kept those coal fires burning brightly. She was a grand old lady, doing all the cleaning and keeping the classrooms tidy by herself, not like it is today where they have several cleaners to do the job.

At this age I recall us children being taken for walks along the canal towpath if we had a cold or chest trouble, and one period when I had the whooping cough – that meant going twice a day 'to blow away the germs'.

I remember Christmas and the times when we each hung our stocking (one of Dad's long woolly socks) on the bed rail. Christmas mornings were lovely, finding our goodies: a few nuts, toffees, an orange, apple and a few items sticking out of the top, a celluloid doll. Sometimes Joyce would get the black one and me the lovely pink one. The following year we each had *vice versa*. Perhaps there would be a game of snakes and ladders or ludo – I know we had one or the other each.

These were lovely times, but one year I wasn't asleep when both Mother and Father crept in to fill our stockings. I was peeping and that was the end of Father Christmas for me.

We children spent many happy hours during nice weather playing shop. Our 'money' was broken china, with different sizes for halfpennies, pennies. threepennies and sixpences. Shillings were coloured pieces. We made mud pies and used daisy heads for decoration. There was also the whip and top, skipping rope and hop scotch played by marking six squares with chalk and kicking a flat stone from one square to the other, by hopping on one leg. We also had large hoops rolled along with a stick. During the winter time we were kept entertained by my dad between teatime and bedtime. He would play his mouth organ, concertina or perhaps the gramophone, that had a huge trumpet horn. We also listened to a story or went through our 10 times tables most nights.

Winter seemed to be the only time we saw much of Dad, because he went to work well before six o clock in the mornings, and although it was dark when he came home about 6.15pm he could at least spend some time with us before we went to bed. It was very different in the summer – there was always work on the farm until very late so we would be in bed by the time he got home. My mother had to help with the milking in the late afternoon, that meant Joyce and I went to our lady carers. Joyce was looked after by Mrs Atherton and I went to Mrs Robinson. We stayed there until my mother returned from her work. For this job they each received 9d each a week. We were never left alone at home.

The Robinsons had five children, one boy, Noel, and four girls, Gladys, Bertha, Winifred and Eva – but only the two younger ones were at home. By this time the other ones were working and 'living in' as it was called.

Mrs Robinson had worked at the munitions factory at Gadbrook during the First World War, and her son Noel, along with Eli Eyres next door, had joined the Army, though they were barely sixteen years of age. They joined under false pretences by pretending they were older. I'm glad to say they went through the four years without injury and both lived to be a very good age. They were such brave boys.

The Robinsons became a second family to me, and although I was 'ruled' and they were very strict, I loved them very much.

CHAPTER TWO

A Ghost at Gadbrook

*My mother and a friend Alice at the back
door of the Parrys' Shipbrook Hill Farm*

When I was about six years old, a couple, Mr and Mrs Copeland and their baby Mary, came to live with us. I learned later it was because they were homeless and had asked my parents to give them shelter. They had only been with us a short while, perhaps nine months, when little Mary became ill and within a week or two "she went to heaven", as my mother told us, and "she was with Jesus". It was a sad time but Joyce and I were taken to see her each night to kiss her goodnight and say "God bless". You see there was no chapel of rest in those days and if anyone passed away they were kept at home until the funeral. It never troubled us because it was the custom to do this and you had no fear of death. The Copelands lived with us for quite a while and then they moved to Rudheath.

When I was six years old I got scarlet fever and was taken to the isolation hospital in Hartford Road, Davenham. I have never forgotten the smell of the broth we were given to drink because our throats were too sore to eat solid food. Scarlet fever was very contagious and our visitors were not allowed inside the wards to visit us; they had to stay outside the windows.

I wasn't happy there and one day I got out through a window and was running as I thought home, but I was going the wrong way and the nurses caught me. How well I remember that day. I could hear the cuckoo calling in the woods and the sun was shining. I was kept in hospital for six weeks which was the limit for scarlet fever.

My mother arrived to take me home when I was better and my friend Ella Eyres who lived up the road from us came with her. We had Mr Whitehead's taxi, the canvas hood was folded back and there were big brass lamps on the front. My mother's hat was held on by a chiffon scarf tied under her chin, we must have looked very grand. It was the first time I had been in a motor car.

The first thing I did when I arrived home was to walk round the garden, and it was a sight that has stayed with me seventy-nine years. I marvelled all the different vegetables my dad had in rows: broad beans, peas, celery and potatoes, it was a lovely sight. The raspberries, gooseberries and blackcurrants were all doing well.

A couple of weeks after I came home another lady and gentleman came to see my parents, begging to be allowed to come and live with us. They were desperate for a home. They had a little boy called Frankie, who was about a year and a half old. He was a lovely child and my parents took them in straight away.

Their names were Mr and Mrs Tom Allen. We all seemed like one big happy family and time went on. Mr Allen was a painter and decorator, and worked for a man in Northwich.

Often work was slack and he would spend time doing the garden for my dad, as he never had a lot of time to spare.

When Frankie was about three years old he got meningitis, and the poor darling passed away. Joyce and I went through the same routine as we had done with baby Mary, going in to kiss him goodnight. We had known him longer and he was like a little brother to us.

Things settled down, and on August 1, 1923 Mrs Allen had a baby girl. They called her Joyce and after two and a half years they had another baby girl named Margaret. We loved those children and in our own way helped to look after them. Sometimes I walked to Forest Street, Northwich (now pulled down) to buy a bottle of "Mothers Friend", a mixture made up by a woman who lived there. It was for babies who suffered from wind, a common ailment with them. It was sixpence for a big medicine bottle full. The remedy you bought at the chemist, called "Nurse Harvey's", did the same job but was more expensive.

While the Allens lived with us he and my dad used to have a flutter on the Sunday newspaper football coupon and my dad asked Mr Allen to post it for him. One week Dad came to check his copy and found he had won £1000. I can't now remember how it came about, but Mr Allen found the envelope my dad had given him to post in his coat pocket.

You can imagine what that money would have meant to my parents. Mr Allen was so very upset that he had forgotten to post it. I can see Dad now. He put his hand on Tom's shoulder and said: "Forget it, Tom, it's one of those things that happens. What we don't have, we don't miss."

You will find it hard to believe but this happened again a couple of years later. This time my mother gave me the penny ha'penny stamp money, which had been left to post the coupon, so that I could use it to buy a pint of paraffin oil on my way home from school. The letter was left on the sideboard. It was right again and Dad would have received £500. His words this time were: "Well, we had to have the oil for the lamp."

That was my dad, he never blamed anyone for anything.

Mr and Mrs Allen stayed with us for a couple more years and they then went to live at Barnton, and although both parents are long gone, we are still friends with Joyce and Margaret.

We were without lodgers after that and life went on. We were very happy. I recall the farmer lending my dad the pony and trap to take the four of us to Northwich on a Friday night to do the shopping. My dad would stable the pony at the Angel Hotel in the Bull Ring, and if it was a wet night Mum and Dad would go to the market, and Joyce and I would be left in the care of Miss Edwards, the daughter of the couple who kept the hotel.

We were taken to their living quarters on the top floor and Miss Edwards would read stories to us. She often told us the story about herself as a child. Her parents kept the Crewe Arms Hotel at the time and a wonderful thing had happened. Queen Victoria had stayed there with her staff and lady in waiting, and Miss Edwards, then a little girl, had got

The Angel Hotel, Bull Ring, Northwich (now demolished)

15

into Queen Victoria's room and was trying on the Queen's bonnet, when the lady in waiting caught her. We loved that story and I am so glad I have remembered it all these years.

When the weather was fine, Joyce and I were taken round Peacock's market and on the public market called the pig bank. This was a treat – in the winter it was illuminated by lights hanging on the sides of the stalls. The toffee stall had all sorts of boiled sweets, pear drops, humbugs, striped balls and lots of names I can't remember, then there was the Devon toffee, plain or brazil nut on trays with a small hammer to break it. My dad always bought half a pound of mixed boiled and half a pound of the Devon, and it lasted a whole week.

We would also visit Dad's cousin's mug stall. He sold anything from a jerry chamberpot to a tea cup, and we thought he was a magician. He would place dinner plates all up his arm and switch them about saying something like: "Who will give me £2, 30 bob, £1, 10 bob....?" and so this went on and they were sold for about five shillings. We were fascinated by it. His name was Mr Poynton. I think some descendants had a china stall in Northwich market until recently.

Near the market there were lodging houses for homeless men and women, who paid ninepence a night to stay there.

We never had a holiday staying at the seaside, only days out. New Brighton was a favourite, there was a funfair at Bellevue and we paid the odd visit to Blackpool. I only ever remember my dad coming to Blackpool once and we had a ride along the front in an open carriage. He never got a holiday when he was farming, it was a seven-day, fifty-two weeks a year job, he even worked at Christmas. During the school holidays we would spend quite a lot of time at Carter's farm or Parry's playing in the fields, or in barns on the bales of straw. That was great fun.

At Carters while mother did her work we used to tie a big metal spoon to a long cane, and go to the ponds in the field and orchard to find duck eggs laid in the water. We collected

Mrs Carter

many of these, and then we would test them in a bowl of water to see if they were fresh or addled.

There was always fresh buttermilk to drink at Carter's as Mrs Carter made a lot of buttermilk. She used to look after the local Cheshire Hunt's fox hound puppies until they were old enough to be trained for the hunt.

I recall many young dogs died of distemper as they did not have the drugs to treat them in those days. It was a sad day when three of them died on the farm, they were called Faith, Hope and Charity. I could go to the place where they were buried today and remember how Marion, Edith, Sam, Joyce and I placed flowers on their grave.

By all accounts there was a ghost at Gadbrook Farm, and both the family and the farm boys who lived in – the Mort boys from Rudheath – believed in Mrs Millington's ghost. My mother also spoke very often of her, she was heard wandering about many a night. The farm boys used to be very scared.

My mother took it all in her stride until one night when she was "sitting up" with Grandma Kinsey, who was more or less in a semi-conscious state. My mum had been up at night with her for about a week, and Mrs Carter used to take her some supper before she went to bed. Mum said she heard her come upstairs and across the room, and thinking she was behind her she said: "Grandma is very poorly. I don't think she will last until morning."

She turned round to see why there was no answer, and

think she will last until morning."

She turned round to see why there was no answer, and there was no one there. It was nearly an hour before her supper was brought up and Mum asked Mrs Carter if she had been upstairs before. She said "no", so mum told her what had happened and they came to the conclusion that Mrs Millington had been on her wanders.

The story went that years before the poor lady had hanged herself from the front staircase banister and a big mark was on it, supposed to have been made by the rope. They said she was a large comely woman and everyone was too sincere about it all for it to have been a made-up story. I wonder, does anyone else remember this lady?

One night I had been up to see Grandma Kinsey, and when I came downstairs with Marion, she said: "Look Nellie, this is the mark left by Mrs Millington's rope."

I felt quite creepy. When I came out Mrs Carter asked me if I would like Sam to take me home. I declined the offer and set off through the lonely farmyard. It was pouring with rain but I had an umbrella. As I went by the big barn door something came down over my head, and my first thought was "Oh! Mrs Millington has got me!" I was rooted to the ground, it seemed ages before I could move my legs, and when I did I ran all the way home. What had happened was that my umbrella hadn't fastened properly when I'd put it up, and the heavy rain had brought it down on my head.

I was thirteen years old when that happened, and I will go back in time and tell you more of the things we did when we were younger.

When our cousins or our friends stayed for a night or two we used to sleep toes to toes. It meant four in a bed but it was lovely, we would be talking half the night.

Aunt Millie and my cousins Dora and Nellie used to visit us nearly every Sunday, and used to walk through Minshall's farmyard and down to Bridge Farm to the Dane bridge. There was a well worn track all the way and it was had the fields between the two farms ploughed up to grow more crops. I don't know what happened to the path afterwards, I think you had to walk round the edge of the field, but I believe it is still a right of way.

During my school days if my mother was working at Gadbrook Farm or Parry's Farm, my sister and I would each go to our respective carer's homes and stay until she came home.

As we got older we used to be allowed to go to the chip shop, the first shop just past the Bull's Head. There was a room upstairs and it held a scrubbed table and a couple of forms, and the walls were covered with green distemper, a sort of lime wash. It is so fresh in my memory. Our dinner was one penny's worth of chips and a halfpenny worth of peas, and we got good value for our money. We would sometimes have these two or three times a week, which was a nice change from our butties.

There was also Miss Clara Whitehead's toffee shop across from the school (now Mr Herbert Warburton's house), where we would spend our weekly halfpenny or penny, depending on what my mother had to spare. We got such things as gobstoppers, aniseed balls, liquorice sticks, love hearts, kayli and a great variety of sweets to choose from. I have Miss Whitehead's toffee scales in my cupboard, Dad bought them at their disposal sale years later.

During those early days I learned many wonderful things. I often stood in the garden and my dad would tell me which direction the wind was blowing, and at different times I have heard the church bells ringing from Middlewich, Witton, Hartford, Davenham and the odd time Great Budworth. It was a great experience: I love the bells to this day.

There were many titbits we used to eat: pig nuts, sour grass, wood sorrel, sweet briar, bread and cheese, hawthorn leaves, hips, beechnuts, chestnuts from Davenham Rectory (the tree by the gate which is still there today), elderberries and wild strawberries, to mention a few.

I got to know the birds and plants. I wonder if the wild arum still grows just along Manor Lane in Whatcroft?

Joyce and I were never allowed to go roaming because there was such a lot of water around Billinge Green: the 'big briny', the 'little briny', the canal, the Dane, the flashes and also Eyre's pit, since filled in by the council with household rubbish – so you can just imagine the concern for the children.

We often played on what we knew as 'Table Mountain', running and rolling in the summer, and sliding in the winter when there was snow. There used to be a lovely sandy beach, as we called it by the River Dane, and we were able to have picnics and paddle in the water just below the river bridge at Shipbrook. It was where a lot of children learned to swim, and there was always someone around to keep their eye on us. I don't ever remember any accidents down there; it was a favourite spot for the families from Davenham.

There is one memory I have when I was very young, about five years old, of a man coming along the road with what we called a 'hurdy-gurdy'. It had a handle to turn for the music to play and a little monkey used to sit on the top. It looked like a box on wheels with pretty flowers painted on it, and he used to push it along like a pram. I wonder where he came from or went to?

Many Saturdays I have walked with Winnie or Eva Robinson to Batty's shop and bakehouse to fetch their mother's shopping. We went down Shurlach Lane to the Farmer's Arms and turned left. The shop was in Middlewich Road near to Agecroft Road. That again was all in a day's work.

We often went to town via the Danefields and came out by the Vicarage, where the Reverend Maitland Wood lived at one time. Another way was over the church fields by Davenham church to the children's home on Leftwich Green and down Brockhurst Hill. Whichever way you went it was a long walk. The only people we ever met going via

Danefields were the farm workers or the Catholic priest. The name "Father Craig" – or "Creagan" – seems to strike a bell in my memory. He loved that walk.

If I'm right he was the priest who eventually had a small wooden bridge built over the brook that we had to cross by stepping stones. It was done to help all the walkers. I wonder if it is still there, I haven't been that way for many years.

Most Sundays, Aunt Millie and my cousins Emily, Annie, Dora and Nellie Clark came from Moulton via the fields, through Minshull's farm yard down to Bridge Farm where Mr and Mrs George Parry and family lived, and on to the road by the Dane bridge.

They would stay for tea which was butties, stewed apple or rhubarb, or whatever what was in season – winter meant bottled fruit with custard. Then came the fruit cake or madeira, which was lovely, and then we would go to their house usually on a Saturday night. These days are still remembered by the few of us that are left, as this routine went on for many years.

CHAPTER THREE

My Schooldays

*My sister Joyce, Patty Atherton, me and Dora Clark pictured
around 1922 – with Joyce's dolls' pram*

I didn't find my schooldays very exciting. It seemed
that as we did not belong to the so-called 'Village
Set', we were not encouraged the same as other children, and speaking recently to a few of my country friends,
they also believe this to be true. We always got the blame for
anything that went wrong.

I remember some instances when I got into trouble. I went
home for my dinner one day and that meant running most
of the way. Anyway, I was halfway home when a very big
vehicle passed me, it turned out to be a fire engine. I had
never seen one before: there were men hanging onto the
sides and they wore big helmets. I hurried on and found it
had stopped at Mrs Carter's farm at the top of Shipbrook

Hill. The farm roof was burning and the firemen would not let me go past. It was late when I got home and my mother was on the lookout for me. She gave me a butty and I hurried back to school. I was very late and the teacher Miss Horton would not believe my story about the fire. She gave me several strokes of the cane on my hand.

When my friends and I went home after school they were astonished to see the damage at the farm, and said it was not fair that I had been punished.

The next morning the fire was the main topic of conversation and my friends told the teacher that I had spoken the truth. There was no apology, or saying: "I am sorry I gave you the cane." That was unheard of, it was all taken for granted.

Once when I was off school with tonsillitis my school friends, who also lived at Shipbrook, brought me a bunch of daffodils. They said they had gathered them from the little wood by the Rectory. My mother put them in water and said it was very thoughtful of them. On the visits each night that second week of my illness, the children had been telling me about a little dog. They said it was sitting on a stump of wood at the bottom of the Dane riverbank and they thought it was waiting to catch water rats. Anyway, on the Monday morning I was better and went to school. We all got as far as the river bridge, and the first thing the children did was to look to see if the dog was gone. There was a shout of "Oh, it's still there!" I looked down and was very shocked at what I saw. I said: "You're all blind! That dog has got a rope round its neck and it's fastened to something in the water. I'm not going to school until I've got it out."

They went on and I, having been taught not to go near water by myself, went to Mr Gregory's small farm and asked him for a rake. I asked if he could come to help me as the bank was very steep. This he did and I climbed down as far as I could, and managed to get the long rake round the rope. This I pulled and slowly got the little terrier up the bank.

23

There was no wonder it was thin and nearly starved to death. The object it was tied to was a drainpipe, and this had sunk down thus holding the poor little mite fast. Somehow it had managed to get onto a tree stump and that had saved it from being drowned.

We walked back to the farm where Mr Gregory looked after and fed the dog until I collected it on my way home at four o' clock.

I then went on to school. My reward was ten good strokes of the cane and a telling off for being late. On another occasion I saved a spaniel from the same river, but this time it had been pegged down on top of the bank to either starve or to be picked up by someone taking a walk through Target Meadow.

Instead of going home I turned back and walked to the police station in Northwich and told them what had happened. I explained that I had been on my way home from school at 4pm, and that my mother would be wondering where I was. While this was going on a police officer walked in, and said: "That dog belongs to Mr So and So in Whalley Road."

They weren't interested at all as to how I would get back, so I took the dog to the house. I'd never heard of the RSPCA, I'm speaking of 75 years ago. Anyway, I walked back to Shipbrook and my mother gave me a good telling off. She said I should have taken the dog home instead of walking all that way. Although I did get a good love afterwards – she said it was for my kind deed, and she was glad to see me safe. I would probably have got a certificate for that today!

But back to the story of the daffodils...

The morning I returned to school at the start of assembly, we had a visitor. It was the Reverend Sandars, and Mr Smith said: "Good morning, what can I do for you?"

"I have come to see who has had the daffodils out of my garden," replied the Rector.

He turned to all us children and said: "I know by the footprints that it's children."

All went quiet, and after a while my friend Patty put up her hand and said: "Please Sir, Nellie Whalley had your daffodils."

My, oh my! I was hauled to the front of the class, and asked why had I not owned up and told the truth. I know I had my flowers from the children, but I hadn't gathered them. I don't believe for one minute to this day that any of us realised that the wood was the Rector's garden. Anyway I did try to explain how it had come about but no one would listen. I was branded as having told a lie and punished by Granny Horton with a wooden blackboard duster. With this I was hit on my back and shoulders, then I had to stand in a corner with a slate, on which I had to write "I have told a lie."

That evening when my mother was giving us our nightly wash, she asked me what had I been up to. Was it fighting, or how come my back was all bruised? I was very reluctant to say, but was told I could not go to bed until she had got to the bottom of it, and in the end I told her what had happened.

The next few minutes she had me dressed and my coat on.

"Come along," said Mother, "we are going to see the Rector."

I was walked to the Rectory. Mother rang the bell. The parlourmaid opened the door, and very haughtily asked: "What do you want?"

"I want a word with the Rector," demanded my mother, and the maid closed the door, saying: "Wait there."

When she came back she took us to a room lined with many books. I learned later it was the study. After a while the Rector came in, and mother explained why she had brought me to see him.

She stripped my clothes down and said: "Take a good look at that!"

I understand by that time my shoulder was quite discoloured, and he was very shocked by this. I was then dressed and he told me he would look into this matter, and not to worry. So we walked all the way back to Shipbrook.

The next morning we had just settled down in class, when in walked the Rector. I could see that Mr Smith was surprised to see him. After a few words the Rector said loudly: "I have come to see who really did take my daffodils, and I shall stay until I hear the right story."

All was quiet, and then my friend eventually put her hand up and told him what had really happened.

I think all would have been well, but I was called out to the front, Granny Hortton was asked to show my bruises to the whole class, and the Rector said: "This is the punishment Nellie got yesterday, and I am not pleased about it."

I felt dreadful standing there, but I never got an apology for it. Anyway on the way home that night my friend chalked something nasty about me on the Rectory wall. This meant the Rector was back at school to find the culprit, saying: "I'll stop here until he or she owns up."

My friend did so this time, and she was told to take a bucket of water and scrubbing brush, to scrub the words off. That meant we didn't speak to each other for a few days.

Now, at 85 and 86 years old, we are the best of friends, and the other day when she called to see me we had a good laugh at the incident. I told her it would go down in my story.

Every morning we started with assembly, morning prayers and hymns, and then went to our classrooms for lessons in the following subjects which were shared out to different days: arithmetic, English, composition, history, geography, nature study, hygiene, sewing, Scripture, singing and games (once a week) – which was hockey or rounders. For these two I remember the first playing field being at Eaton Hall Farm on the right of the driveway, the village cricket green was also down there once. Next we went to Davenham Hall Park and played games there. I believe there is still a bit of the old cricket field fence in Eaton Lane after all these years.

I loved being out at games. I was good at sewing and hygiene, and got a certificate for the latter, but nature study was my favourite.

Davenham School (right) and the toffee shop, near group of people (left).

When I started at Davenham School, Mr Earlam was headmaster, Miss Johnson was headmistress, Miss Hewitt took the baby class, followed by Mrs Rose, and later in higher classes there were Miss Haughton, Miss Gladys Foster and Mr Merrick. Another teacher, Mr Evans, left to go to Little Budworth School as headmaster. Then Mr Earlam and Miss Johnson retired. Mr Harry Smith came as headmaster, and Mr Dean joined the staff. That's how it was until I left.

We weren't very old when we were taught to darn our stockings and underwear, and put patches on the elbows of our blouses. We also darned our jumper elbows. There is no shame in a darn, it's a work of art if done properly. You will hear about a repair to a pair of stockings later on in my life, and then you will understand what I mean.

Time went on and we were old enough to start cookery lessons. This meant walking to Moulton School, because there were no facilities at Davenham School. Each Thursday morning we went across the fields and up Minshull's Drive to Mereheath, and then along Jack Lane into Moulton. Our first teacher was Miss Simmcock, and then we later had Miss Pitts whose father was the vicar at Hartford church. Our cookery lessons went on for two years, and I must admit

27

my schoolmates and I had some very happy times there – Doreen Evans, Evelyn Yarwood, Beatty Dean, Daisy Mears, Marjorie Mears (cousins), Patty Atherton, Louie Crimes and myself, to name but a few.

After we had our lunch about four of us used to go for a walk as far as the Tank Bridge over the main railway line running from London to Scotland. It was called Tank Bridge because there was a water tank nearby. We would watch so many goods wagon trains and so many passenger trains go along, and then we knew it was time to go back to class. One day we must have missed one and eventually we thought it was a long break. We hurried back and oh my goodness, the afternoon was well gone, and we were unable to do our baking.

We were each given strokes of the cane and made to stand in different parts of the room. I'm afraid our reaction was to start laughing, and that meant more of the cane. I can't count the strokes we got that day but it did not cure us. I had to own up to my parents what had happened, because there were no scones for my dad's tea that day. We got a good telling off, and were told never to go near the railway again.

We used to visit Aunt Millie's at Moulton, during the school holidays. It meant staying there for a few days, and playing with Dora and Nellie's friends. We would go up to the 'rec' playing field and have a lovely time. The hedges had lovely 'cops', and we used to make our playhouses in the gaps using lace curtains for drapes. A couple of us would make each house and be neighbours, Vera Dutton, Jessie Allcock, Nellie Birkenhead, Annie Cookson, Jessie Brereton, Ada Stubbs, Dora Clark, Nellie Clark, Elsie Buckley, Molly Hewitt, Joyce my sister and myself. These are some of the girls I remember. Sadly one or two have passed away but those who remain still remember those happy times. After our busy days we were put to bed toes-to-toes as at our house.

We got such a great deal of pleasure out of so little and never seemed to be dissatisfied.

Some of the business people I remember at Moulton were Dearden's coal yard on Main Road, the bakehouse, Darlington's in Chapel Lane, Winstanley's toffee shop, Wilson's clog and shoe shop, the Co-Op, Buckley's haberdashery, clothes and hat shop, Whitlow's grocery, Buckley's greengrocer's, Hardman's butchers (they also had a slaughterhouse on the backs of Regent Street), a couple of chip shops and some newsagents.

My mother bought Joyce and myself clogs from Wilson's, and I remember the metal tips on the toes. We used to play in them and wear them to save our school shoes. It is sad to think all these customs have died out – perhaps one day they will be the fashion again.

I must now get down to the basics of our lives at Shipbrook. My mother started her days by seeing to our breakfast of Quaker Oats, and we would be sent to our 'second homes' until school time. Then she would go to Parry's to clean all the milk cans and coolers, and the large tankards that had been returned from Manchester. This done, it was all-day washing at Carter's farm on Mondays, ironing on Tuesdays, and then two or three cleaning days. During this time our house was kept spotless and the washing and cooking was done. She had no modern washer or vacuum cleaner, it was all rubbing, scrubbing and polishing. No wonder there was such a thing as chapped hands. You will have a shock when I tell you of a well-known remedy for that: soaking your hands in urine. Yes, that is quite true! There were many strange remedies in those days to get relief from pain and different ailments. Urine was even used as an eye-bath!

At night mother prepared the porridge from Quaker Oats, which were proper rolled oats. The big iron saucepan was almost filled with water and the oats were added with a pinch of salt, stirred well and then brought to the boil. The porridge was then put in the great big oven attached to the

29

fire grate, and in the morning it was ready to eat. We always had plenty of milk on it. Sometimes we would have bread and milk, 'pobs' we called that. It was our choice of breakfast. We mostly took butties for our dinner at school, or, as I have said earlier, we went to the chip shop. During the week our meal was later, when Dad finished work.

What we had at different times included oxtail stew, ham shank pea soup (which was a meal in itself), pressed tongue, and – at Mrs Robinsons – boiled cow's udder. This was the only dish I could never take to, although I did have to eat it because there was no such thing as left-overs. It was unheard of, you would hear these words: "Get that down, there's many a child would be glad to eat it", and down everything went. We also had potato pie, neck chop stew and, for a change, stewing meat off the leg, tripe and onions, liver and onions, and eggs galore. I often swallowed raw eggs just like oysters – they were lovely! We had ham and pork sometimes, because we always seemed to have a pig called Joey, kept in a sty in the garden. Besides all these things my dad would often bring home a rabbit, so again it was rabbit stew or pie, both lovely.

The puddings, or as we called them, "afters", were stewed apples, pears, rhubarb, raspberries, loganberries, or these made into pies. One popular pie I never hear of now was rice and currant pie. It was made in a deep enamel soup plate, lined with short pastry and filled with boiled rice and currants, and had a pastry top. This was cooked in the oven until the pastry was done, and was eaten hot or cold.

We always had fruit through the winter because Mother bottled each kind as it was season. She also made jams and marmalade, so that we never went short. At Christmas several Christmas puddings were made, and we saved the silver threepenny bits, as we called them. One of these for each member of the family was put in the puddings. The washing boiler was used to cook them for a few hours. They kept edible for years – they were just stored, used as needed and that's how it went on. The oldest were used each year so that the new ones could age. Vegetables were also used, including red cabbage and onions, to make piccalilli and chutney.

What with the flitch of bacon, hams and all the items mentioned above, the pantry was a sight to be remembered. Mrs Robinson and my mother always made the most of what the garden produced by seeing that nothing went to waste. They also made their own bread – we only got it from the van if we ran out of homemade. I don't remember all these things being done by the other two neighbours, perhaps that's why mother never sent our next door neighbour away when she often came round to 'borrow' some item of food. Anyway, my mother used to say: "It will come back some way."

I never saw anything returned myself.

The cooks in the halls around used to sell beef dripping at 9p a pound, and it was lovely on toast. You see, in the big houses beef was a daily joint and unlike today there was always layers of fat in the meat, and when it was cooked you had the lovely dripping. When poured into jars it used to set, and always had a thick layer of lovely brown jelly at the bottom. It's definitely not the same as today.

You were lucky to know a cook who was able to supply you: it all helped and dripping was used often instead of butter. You'd get a slice of bread covered with beef dripping, a pinch of salt on top and it beat the lot. It was lovely on toast.

By the way, mother cured her hams with block salt and salt petre to go in the bone joints. Block salt was used to cure the bacon. You didn't get a pint of water coming out of the bacon in your pan when you cooked it, like you do today. It was pure 'dip' as we called it. You could eat many dip butties, and you'd had a good meal.

We did manage to keep a pig right through the 1939-45 war, and for a while afterwards, so that helped out the rations. I do know that during the war rules were very strict and an official checked the amount of livestock a cottager could keep. It all had to be accounted for.

CHAPTER FOUR

Second-hand clothes

Mrs Robinson at her cottage door

Often at the end of my mother's working week and when the time came to be paid, she was told: "We haven't the money to pay you this week, so it will have to be some of the girls' grown out-of clothes."

These were accepted because there was no choice, but Mrs Carter's two daughters were always well dressed. They had their clothes from Bratt and Evans, and I later learned that Mrs Carter's sister had a second-hand shop in London, and dealt with the upper classes. She often sent clothes along for Marion and Edith. We in turn got these, so we were well dressed in the "London fashion", no less.

Today people go to charity shops, so it's really no different, but I must say I was always embarrassed by wearing these hand-me-downs. This was not helped by an incident at school one day. My desk mate and friend, Evelyn Yarwood, said to me in class: "I like your frock, Nellie, what shop did your mother buy it?"

"Oh," I answered, "it was part of my mother's wages. They told her that they had no money to pay her."

The next thing Mr Smith bellowed out at me, and asked what I was talking about. I was reluctant to say, and I was hauled out in front of the class and made to repeat my conversation. I never did forgive Mr Smith for that, I felt so degraded. I had my pride.

Anyway, quite a few years later a very strange thing happened. I was working at Merebank House and I asked the lady if she could find me some oddments for the church rummage sale. Amongst the clothes she gave me was a lovely cream pleated skirt, and I must admit I wished I had one like it. I went to the sale hoping to buy it, but it was not there. You'll never believe where I next saw it, along with other items at different times. Yes – being worn by Mr Smith's eldest daughter! His wife was one of the helpers and organisers of the stalls. You can't imagine how elated I was, it didn't matter to me any more that I hadn't got the skirt myself. I had got my own back after all that time, and the headmaster's daughter was wearing rummage sale clothes. I was more proud that my mother had worked hard for my clothes. To you it may seem very catty to feel like that, but not to me. I always remember my school days and the way we were treated at times.

When I was quite young my mother bought a piano, and I had music lessons for the next three years. One hour each week at Miss Golden's, who lived in London Road opposite to Green Lane. My mum paid her 1/6d for each lesson and the music books used to be 1/3d. I shall never know why this went on so long. You see, I habitually played by ear – in other words I didn't bother to read the notes on the sheets of music.

They were still determined I should play the piano, so I was taken away from Miss Golden and went to Mrs Williams of Peter Street, just down Manchester Road. This meant going on the Dodger train at 1.20pm and returning at 4pm. There I had my fingers rapped with a ruler many times. I went there for nearly another three years and there was very little improvement, so eventually I stopped. All my mother's hard-earned money had been wasted.

About half way through this learning time there was a agreement between my mother and Mrs Robinson that the piano should be moved to their house, and they would see that I did an hour's practice every night after school. The real truth was Mrs Robinson had always fancied the piano, and believe you me, it never came home again!

If by any chance I stopped playing during that hour – to look through the window at my friends having fun on the road outside – I was made to play extra time until my full hour was up.

Another punishment I had for playing too many jokes, answering back (which wasn't very often) or whatever, was that I was made to sit on a kitchen chair with my back very straight, and no bending or relaxing. Behind me on the wall was the big clock with a very loud tick, on the other wall was a huge picture of Hawarden castle. I often sat there for an hour at a time, and the tick of that clock haunts me to this day. What terrible memories – it wasn't as if I had done any-thing really bad.

The Robinsons were good people and cared well for me, but it was just that there was always such strict discipline in that house.

Don't get me wrong and think it was all bad – I did have some fun. When the weather was nice, Eva and I used to play our own form of tennis in the garden with a racket and ball, and we would go for walks. I was allowed to do that because Eva was so much older than me and a responsible girl.

I remember the time all the girls, Ella, Eva, Patty, Lizzie, Nancy, Joyce, myself and the Gough boys, three or four of them, decided to have a May Day. The mothers must have got together because I recollect our fancy long frocks, the Queen, and her head-dress made from fresh flowers. Her train was a white lace curtain.

The event was held at the top of Eyre's L-shaped field and our procession walked along the road, past the cottages and then all the way up the field. I remember quite a few people being there, but other than our parents I don't know who they were. There was a big trestle table laid out with jam butties, egg butties, cakes and homemade lemonade to drink afterwards. I can't remember the outcome of it as I wasn't very old.

When I between nine and twelve years old, at Halloween time we used to go soul-caking. That meant taking a basket, after tea and going round the local farms – Worth's, Stubb's, Parry's, Carter's, Eyre's and Frith's. We would sing songs and one ended "If you haven't got a penny a ha'penny will do, if you haven't got a ha'penny, God bless you." Our reward would be mostly fruit, and sometimes the odd scone or fairy cake, which were very welcome. We also got eggs.

I remember the last time we went to the farm on the top of Shipbrook Hill. As we were singing, the Mr Carter's window above the front door opened and we had what we originally thought was water thrown all over us – he was that kind of man. But by the smell on our clothes it was decided that it had been a jerry full of wee!

We carried a shippon lamp to light us on our way, and we would go into Stubb's field and root in the turnip hog for a couple of turnips. Someone would have a pen knife and we all sat down on the straw, peeled away and tucked into pieces of our spoils.

We seemed to grow up with turnips. We had them chopped up with carrots and boiled as a vegetable. They were used in stews, and if we had a bad cough my mother would grate a turnip very fine and put it in a big deep soup plate, sprinkle it with brown sugar, leave it over night, and the dose we got was two teaspoonfuls of the liquid that was made. It always did us good and it was pleasant to drink. Joyce and I would eat the remains of the remedy. It was lovely grub!

Other times I have known us to go behind Gregory's Farm and into the little wood where there was always a turnip hog, and root away until we had one. We would peel it and share the pieces. This came to an end when Mr Gregory caught us there one day, and my did we get a fright. We never opened a hog again.

Really we were no different from the children of today, only we got into mischief in different ways. We would tie the door knobs of houses in Church Street, Davenham, then knock loudly and run off. This was usually done on the way home from school.

If we ran out of paraffin oil at home it meant taking a can and leaving it at Mottershaw's shop, which stood on the corner in the village where the little garden is now. The can was then collected when we went home at four o'clock. We also often bought Dad his packet of Woodbine cigarettes, which cost twopence for a packet of five and a box of matches for one penny. I remember this box had a picture of Captain Webb on it and the manufacturers were Bryant and May.

Twice we lit bonfires, one in the field just past the two bungalows and the other in the hollow of a large tree. We ran away from this terrified when we saw the smoke coming out of the top – we didn't know for a long time that it was hollow all the way up and very rotten. That was the last time we lit fires, we learned our lesson.

One day I did light one of the cigarettes, when the other children dared me. I took one puff and that was the end of smoking for me. That was well over seventy five years ago.

Over the years I remember a most welcome visitor to our house was the Reverend George Sandars, usually on a Saturday. He used to sit by the fire and more often than not there was a cake or bread cooking in the oven. He would say: "Oh what a good smell, I love sitting here."

He talked to us about our schooling and to my mother about work – how she managed to cope with it and getting us to church when she could – and while this was going on he was served with a cup of tea and a piece of cake.

He would walk miles and visit the cottages and farms as far as Whatcroft Lane and King Street. I think as young as we were, even we felt the benefit of his visits.

There was something I never understood. Only my mother and Mrs Robinson went out to work, the other two neighbours didn't. The lady from Whatcroft Hall, Mrs Baerline, was very good to our next door neighbour, she used to send clothes for them that her own children had grown out of. Their dad was a sick man and he passed away. All of those children worked hard and got decent jobs. I pay tribute to them. My mother and their mum were very close friends.

I was quite a bonny girl and at around twelve or thirteen years old my feet had grown with the rest of me, and I took size seven shoes. When my mother took me to Mr Griffith's shoe shop in Church Street he said it was difficult to get big sizes for girls, but he would do his best. It was over a week before I went to try on my new shoes. What a shock I had. They were black, laced up, with a toe cap. They were for boys! I went mad and said that I would never wear boys' shoes, but in the end I had to give in because it was them or nothing. Who would have thought that type of shoe would be fashionable seventy odd years later, and all the teenagers would be clumping round wearing them! I have never forgotten how degraded I felt at having such clumsy shoes.

About that time and for a number of years later, I was favoured with Mrs Carter's cast-off shoes as they were my size, and again formed part of my mother's wages for the work she did. It turned out that our neighbour took the same size, so often on Saturdays or whenever, she wore my shoes to go to town. She also borrowed a new coat of my sister's to go out in.

One day she split a seam down the back because really it was too small for her. Anyway, she was offered the damaged coat for ten shillings and she declined the offer. Once when the daughter wore Joyce's shoes to go to Davenham, they were on the way home and a car driver (cars were seldom seen) took the corner too close and ran over Nancy's toes. She wasn't hurt because the shoes were far too big! The man stopped, gave Nancy half a crown and drove off. We never did find out who it was. I remember Joyce saying: "I should have had the money because they were my shoes that were run over."

One of our treats at school was a day out during the summer to Bostock Hall. Captain France Hayhurst used to put on a big tea party for all the schoolchildren. We were taken to the hall on a farm lorry, pulled by a lovely big horse. My dad was one of the men who had one lent by Mr Tom Parry, and Dad would dress the horse up with lovely braids and shiny horse brasses, he would walk and lead the horse by holding the reins. Other farmers also lent lorries: you can imagine the lovely parade. Just a plod, plod and the children's voices raised in excitement; no cars to get in the way with their noise.

We went through the big wrought iron gates at the first lodge, and down the long tree-lined drive. There is no entry that way now, but you can still follow its course by the avenue of lovely trees growing there.

I used to love these outings because it was so beautiful in the gardens, with their lawns and flower beds, roses and a lake covered in water lilies. Miss Rennie, the young daughter of the captain, used to be brought out by Miss Spiller, her nanny, to walk amongst us. I don't know why, but she always made a beeline for me. She was such a lonely child, never knowing her mother, who had died when Miss Rennie was a baby.

There was always a strict eye kept on her by Miss Spiller, who to us seemed to be quite old. There would be small swing boats for us to ride in, and Miss Rennie used to beg for me to take her for a ride. This only happened once, she was never allowed another one. I used to think she was treated like a china doll. Anyway, after games and a grand tea we were got ready for the journey back. It was the end to a lovely day for another year.

When she was old enough, Miss Rennie's education was shared with the children at Whatcroft Hall. They were the Baerlines, and their instruction was taken one term at Bostock and one at Whatcroft. The poor girl didn't seem to mix with anyone else. I christened her the 'poor little rich girl'. I don't know what happened to the Baerlines but they moved away, and Dr Stirling, the eye specialist from Manchester, bought the hall and lived there. He retired later and his great hobby was growing orchids. I believe he had a wonderful collection.

How times have changed. Both halls with their barns and outbuildings are now big housing projects, and in Bostock's instance, the hall has been made into flats and new houses have been built in the grounds. To my way of thinking, it was a very sad end for two beautiful halls. I'm afraid the children of today will never see or be able to enjoy our heritage. Gone are the sights and the freedom of lovely walks through the park at Whatcroft Hall. The lodges have been sold and there is no way through the park. You have to go via King Street to get to Richardson's farm, and I believe the keeper's cottage was pulled down long ago.

I can't ever see modern children playing in Bluebell Wood, down Whatcroft Lane or by the stream which runs through it, where cowslips, primroses, bluebells, campion, cuckoo flower, harebells, lady smock and marigolds ran riot, not forgetting the celandines, coltsfoot and wild arum. I think it is all unspoiled. There used to be a lot of white and blue violets, but by the time I was leaving school they had become very scarce, because Molly Hill used to dig them up and transplant them into their garden at Church Street, Davenham! I think it was wrong to do that. I remember so well that all of us children were taught by our parents to take a great interest in the wild life.

Every year we waited for the swallows, swifts and cuckoos, and we seemed to know by instinct where all the different birds would nest. Wrens and robins always built in the hedge 'cops' along by Carter's orchard and on the other side of the road. In that hedge we found the nests of blackbirds, thrushes, chaffinches and hedgesparrows. Throughout the nesting season we watched and waited for the day the eggs would hatch. Numbers would vary from three to six. The wren and other small birds often laid more eggs in their nests, and when feeding time came all the parent birds must have flown many miles in search of suitable food for their chicks. They were busy from morning till night: it was a wonderful time.

When I was about ten years old, I remember we had very bad frosts during the winter and our source of drinking water, the pump along the road, was completely frozen up. Even 'the briny', canal and flashes were frozen. People came from miles away to skate on the ice. My dad remembered a natural spring at the back of Whatcroft Wood. He went to check it and found it was still running. It was the only source of water for all those people who used Eyre's pump to get their drinking water. I went with them to that spring and carried as much as I could get in my bucket. It meant us walking to Parry's Farm, down the Cow Lane, along the River Dane, and there at the back of the wood was the spring. It never did freeze up, and a while ago I enquired about it for a talk I was giving. I discovered that it was still running with lovely clear water.

Joyce and I were threatened with what trouble we would be in if we went near the 'ice rinks', as we called them.

However, one night Joyce, Nancy and myself – accompanied by Patty, our one-time neighbour, who by this time was living in the fields behind Manor Far – took a short cut across the fields by the railway. It was so easy to cut across the frozen flashes, a big sheet of water supposed to be bottomless. This we did against all the warnings of danger.

Imagine our horror when there was a noise like a big crack right by us. I learned later that it was the ice sagging. We did not know which way to run. We all ended up in different places at the edge, and I have never been so thankful to feel my feet on solid ground.

To this day, seventy five years later, I have never set foot on ice, even to slide on it, because that night still gives me the creeps when I think about it. Thank God I have lived to tell the story and I have warned many children of the danger of frozen fish ponds.

Nancy, Patty, Joyce and myself seemed to stick together as good pals, and later we got bicycles, if you could call them that. We were lucky to have two brakes, a bell and a pump between us. We never went to school on them but we had such fun around the lanes.

I remember we set out for a ride which was meant to be

Davenham Hall - home of the Russell Allan family

41

just a short trip, and to this day I've never found out how we arrived in Kelsall! On the way we were pushing our bicycles up a hill and we met an elderly man. I said to him: "Can you please tell us where we are?" and the answer sounded like 'Yuckerton'.

We were none the wiser, so we carried on until we came to some houses, and on enquiring were told we were in Kelsall. We were told to turn right at the end of that road and we would get to Hartford.

When we got home we said we had got lost and told Dad what the man on the hill had said. He explained that we had been through Utkinton and the man had been speaking the local dialect. My, what an experience – a "foreign land".

One day we were riding down Whatcroft Lane and as we turned the corner coming down the hill, we came across the Cheshire Hunt hounds and huntsmen. We couldn't pull up and the language those huntsmen used on us was terrible. You see, they thought only they were allowed to be on the road. How we emerged through horses and the pack of hounds I will never know, but we did so without mishap.

We used to take picnics in Rudheath Woods, now called Shakerley Mere. There was only the odd pond amongst all the trees, a lot of silver birches which had lovely graceful branches. We would play a game of hide and seek and run about for ages, then have our picnic. When we came home we used to call at a tiny cottage across from the Common Lane turning at Lach Dennis to get a drink. The lady's name was Mrs Haines, and she was so kind to us. Years later she sold cigarettes to passers-by. Her husband seemed quite old to us, with his whiskers round his chin, and he always seemed to wear corduroy trousers tied below the knee with a piece of baling twine.

My mother also took Joyce and me to a Miss Richmond who lived in a cottage on the corner, opposite to the Duke of Portland. She was asked to make our confirmation dresses out of white silk. I remember we went for a number of fittings before they were finished, and we wore them with pride at our confirmation at Davenham Church in 1928.

I understand Miss Richmond was a sick lady and she died quite young.

During my last year at school my dad had managed to buy us all bicycles, not new but in good condition, and they got us to places. When it was nice, on Sunday evenings now and again my dad and Uncle Walter would take Joyce and me for a run out along Bostock, through Middlewich, along to Sandbach and back home through Holmes Chapel, Byley, Lach Dennis and so home. I loved these outings and recall the stops for refreshment, first at The Military Arms, Sandbach. Joyce and I would sit outside with a glass of lemonade, and the two men had half a pint of mild inside. Our next stop was the Duke of Portland, just a tiny country pub, not the grand place of today. We got to know the land-lady Mrs Edwards very well and she became a friend.

I spend a lot of time awake during the night now I'm older, and to help me pass the long hours I often take a trip down memory lane. I gather baskets of blackberries, and pick mushrooms, or bunches of honeysuckle. I listen to the sky-lark (not heard in real life for a number of years) and you would be surprised how these memories help the night to pass.

It is a regular thing for me to say to my dear husband in the morning: "I've had a lovely time. I went for a walk along the canal last night" or "I've been for a run to Boots Green, I feel better for it."

CHAPTER FIVE
'Between Maid'

Davenham church and Rectory

*E*ventually the time came for my school days to finish and I had to decide about work. I had an interview with Mrs Sandars the rector's wife, and was accepted to start work, living in at the Rectory as a 'between maid'. That meant the beginning of learning to be a cook. My first idea was to be a nurse and I went to see the Matron of Northwich Infirmary. I was told I must wait until I was sixteen years old, and as money was short in those days I could not afford to wait, so I took the alternative and plumped for domestic service when I was fourteen.

This meant leaving behind a loving family and the neighbours who were there to help when help was needed. There were no Government hand-outs in those days.

One thing I remember was the advice I had from Mrs Robinson, Aunt Millie and my mother: "Make sure you get up on time, do as you're told, don't answer back, make sure you do this and that..." It was worse than going to school.

Anyway, I did everything I could to the best of my ability and came through it all. I could not do more than that, as you will see from the following account of my working life.

Gone were my lovely soft feather bed and the pillows all made by my mother, with feathers stripped and stoved to make them clean, and hot oven shelves or house bricks kept specially as bed warmers. Yes, all those comforts were left behind when I had to start to earn a living.

I was fourteen years old on April 2, 1928 and left school on the Friday. Saturday and Sunday I spent at home and on the Monday morning I walked to Davenham Rectory with my suitcase. In it were all the things I possessed, including a hair brush and comb, clothes brush, two small brushes, a tin of black shoe polish to keep my shoes in good order, an alarm clock and what clothes I needed.

I arrived at nine o'clock and was introduced to other staff – Miss Annie Armit, the cook, who was to be my boss, parlourmaid Nellie Tickle and housemaid Kathleen Davies. Kathleen was told to take me to my bedroom which was on the second floor. There I took possession of my uniform. Morning wear was a blue frock and two huge morning aprons with bibs and long straps to go over my shoulders and fasten at the back waist. There was also a stiff white linen cap. Afternoon uniform was a black dress, an apron we called a 'nippy' with a cap to match, just a small band with black velvet threaded through the open work on the edge. Lyon's café waitresses wore the same uniform, hence the name 'nippy'.

When I was dressed I was taken down to the kitchen to be shown what I was expected to do. My duties were explained. I had to rise at six o'clock each morning and in my room was a wash stand holding a large jug and bowl, and soap dish.

The jug had to be kept full of cold water which was carried from the bathroom on the floor below. We emptied the dirty water and cleaned everything up during the time that we had when we washed and changed into afternoon uniform. The bed was made and the room tidied also during this time. When I got down to the kitchen at about ten minutes past six I had to clean out the ashes in the big cooking range, re-lay and light the fire, clean the range with black lead and polish the steel surround with a cloth and cleaning powder. I also had to fill and boil the huge iron kettles and prepare a tray, containing two cups and saucers for a cup of tea, for the cook and parlourmaid. I took this to the top of the house, woke them up and left them to drink their tea.

Back in the kitchen I had to get all the dishes and utensils which Cook needed to prepare the lavish breakfast, for 'up front' as we called it. The Rector and his wife had a big family, with five sons who came home during the school holidays. The choice varied each day, but the menus usually included a choice of kippers, kedgeree, boiled eggs, scrambled eggs, poached eggs on toast, bacon, egg, tomatoes, mushrooms, toast, marmalade, tea and coffee. Cook also made fresh plain scones every morning. All the food was put on a huge sideboard in silver dishes. Some had a container of hot water underneath to keep them warm. I never remember seeing any food returned to the kitchen other than some toast and a few scones!

Strange to say but true, I never remember having any breakfast myself and recently I met a woman who as a girl had followed in the same job, and she said: "Oh yes it's true, we never had time to stop for breakfast."

So I was right.

The parlour maid was in charge of all the silver, and that was washed, polished and kept in her pantry, as it was called. All the dirty plates, china dishes and so on, came back to the kitchen to be washed and stored.

When I had finished washing everything, including the

cook's pans and utensils, it was 9.30am and time for me to go upstairs to help Kath, the housemaid to make the beds, empty slops, and clean the bedrooms and bathrooms. This I did until 11.30am, then it was back to the kitchen to have a drink and a piece of cold toast or a scone, which were the leavings of the 'up front' breakfasts.

Next job was getting all the dishes and utensils out and put handy for Cook to prepare the one o'clock lunch. My job then was to prepare all the vegetables. After lunch and we had eaten, I washed everything up and cleaned the kitchen and scullery, then tidied the servants' hall which was kept clean – but we never had any time to sit in it.

After these jobs were done and for a few days once a month I had to wash personal items belonging to the cook. I wasn't aware that wasn't my job at all and she was taking advantage of me.

It was then time for me to go to my own room and, as I have said, make my bed, get washed and change into my black dress. I often felt like lying on my bed and having a rest, but there was no one else downstairs to get the staff's tea ready.

At 4pm we had to serve afternoon tea, sandwiches and cake for our employers.

After tea it was the same. I washed the dishes and then started to prepare for the 'up front' evening dinner. This consisted of at least three or four courses. Soup, fish, main course – which could be duck, lamb, pheasant, chicken or beef. There was always a choice of vegetables with the main dish, plus dessert, fruit, and coffee. At 10pm a big tray of tea went 'up front'.

I have always marvelled at the amount of food that was eaten.

No wonder the toffs in those days suffered from gout, it's a wonder they could walk at all!

After late dinner it was the same routine, wash up and tidy everywhere ready to start the next morning. One job I had to do before the daily eight o'clock Communion Service was to have the front hall floor washed (Fridays scrubbed), and the front steps cleaned before the Rector went over to the church. My bucket and I had to be out of sight. I don't think I set eyes on the Rector more than twice in the two years I worked there.

Life had most certainly changed for me. The only day that was different was Friday. When I'd washed up the lunch things and cleaned the kitchen and scullery, I had to scrub the long stone floor of the passage that led from the hall to the back door. I was still scrubbing it one Friday when Mrs Sandars came along to feed her fowl. All of a sudden she stopped by me and said: "Get that dress lengthened, you're showing too much leg."

It was already ankle length, so you can imagine how I felt. Anyway, I had my little sewing case with me in my room, so I did the job when I went up to change into my black frock.

Monday was my half day off each week. It was getting on towards 4pm by the time I reached home, and I had to be back inside the Rectory by 9.30pm. Once a month I was supposed to have a full day off, but by the time I had finished washing the breakfast things, tidied my room and got ready,

London Road, Davenham

48

it was about 11am. I set off for home. By the way, it wasn't an extra day off, only my half day lengthened. This time was spent mostly at home. I was so pleased to be with my family. Dad always took me back at night, he would push his bike there and ride it home.

For all this work I received seven shillings and sixpence per week (about 35p in today's money!), which was paid in the total of one pound ten shillings each month. My mother received that and kept me clothed out of it. That was my first year's wages for working seven days a week, 6am until about 10.30-11pm at night. I did get a rise in my weekly income of 1/6d per week for my second year's apprentice-ship.

When you became sixteen years old you had to leave the Rectory because it was time for them to start paying insurance stamps, and as there were plenty of fourteen-year-old school leavers they just changed the between maid to save expense.

The outside staff were gardener, Mr Hand, chauffeur, Mr Hockenull and the gardener cum odd-job boy, who in my time was Walter Thompson. He was replaced at sixteen years of age for the same reason as me. Again, there were plenty of fourteen-year-old lads looking for jobs, who didn't need insurance stamps.

Mr Hand always had a kind word for me. He knew how hard I worked, never having a minute to myself, but of course it was like that in those days. You most certainly earned what little money you got. I kept in touch with Mr Hand and his family until he died in 1941.

We didn't get treated very well by the parlourmaid. She thought she was well above 'below stairs', but now and again I did get a laugh. Once a year, one day was very special. A great number of vicars from the diocese came for the day, it was called 'Silent Day'. There was no talking, just medita-tion until lunch when they all sat down to eat – I remember this so well. There was roast lamb on the menu and that meant me spending ages chopping mint for the sauce: it had to be chopped so fine it was almost dust. Anyway, the lamb was eventually served and parlourmaid Nellie Tickle, all prim and proper, was going round with the sauce and somehow tripped. The sauce went all down a parson's neck, and you can imagine the panic! I was very naughty when I was told of the incident by the housemaid, Kath.

I said: "Well, that knocks her off her pedestal."

In the summer of my first year, 1928, the family rented a huge place in Milford-on-Sea, called Hordle House School. There was the Sandars family of seven, the Rector's brother and his family and also other guests. We, the staff and the extra help they employed, were all sent down by train. It was such a long journey and I remember we were held up in Brockenhurst Station for a while. Everyone was startled by a loud ringing up on the luggage rack, and on investigation it was discovered I was the culprit. It was my alarm clock going off at twenty-five to six, although it was late afternoon. That was the time my clock was set for me to get up each morning. We eventually got to our destination and as soon as we had refreshed ourselves and changed into our uniform, it was back to work. We provided late dinner for the holidaymakers who had travelled by car.

I often think back on that month at Milford-on-Sea. The only time I had off was a visit one night, I'm not sure if it was to Lymington or Christchurch, for a carnival, and a full day with all the staff to the Isle of Wight. We went across the island to Ryde by train, and paid a visit to Carisbrooke Castle. I loved that. After a lovely day we returned by boat to the mainland, and were met by the sons of the family who brought us back to Hordle House in cars. That was called our 'treat'.

We were very busy in the kitchen during that month, and it seemed to me that we never stopped cooking.

One day the Rector's brother, Colonel Sandars, sent a message to the cook saying to congratulate whoever had mashed the potatoes for lunch, as she knew her job and they were lovely. I thought, "That is a feather in my cap," as I did all the vegetables.

I only went down to the private beach belonging to the house once, and in the distance there was a lady dressed in black who had a type of cape over her head. I have often wondered over the years if she could have been a nun. It was so lonely I never went there again.

The month passed quickly and we returned to the Rectory. I was really glad when it came time for my afternoon off, so that I could see my family again. I had missed them so much.

It was then back to the same routine of work, and I had to put in a year's service before I was entitled to a week's holiday. That is when I had a couple of days out. I have one legacy left to me from my first two years scrubbing and cleaning. The marks are still on my knuckles from the segs left by the stone floors, and no amount of cream has ever got rid of them.

$\mathcal{K}$itchen $\mathcal{M}$aid

The centre of Davenham looking down Church Street

*J*ust before I was sixteen years old I began to think of my next post. I heard that Mrs Carver at Hartford Hall wanted a kitchen maid, so I got an interview with the housekeeper, Mrs Dickenson. This was successful and I made arrangements to start at the end of my month's notice at the Rectory. I had very good references from Mrs Sandars so they helped.

Kitchen maid meant one step higher to becoming a fully experienced cook so I was proud to be getting on. Things were quite different at Hartford Hall. There was Mr and Mrs Carver, but they had no family at home, just one daughter who was married to David Sheppard, the curate or vicar at St Martins-in-the-Field. They employed a housekeeper, butler, cook, ladies maid, parlourmaid, housemaid and myself. Outside were chauffeur, gardener and garden and odd job boy. I had different duties from what I had done at the Rectory, and I was in the kitchen all the time. There was no bedroom cleaning – only our own, that I shared with Winnie Smith, the parlourmaid. Mr Hollinshead the butler was Winnie's boss, and Cook was my boss. I had to make all the sauces and custards, and clean and cook all the vegetables.

Here I also skinned rabbits and hares, and plucked game and fowl. This family, as did the Rector's, ate very well – they had a cooked lunch and dinner every day. They were supposed to have lost all their money in the cotton slump and I never understood the size of the house they lived in, and how they could employ all that staff. Words still fail me after all these years. One thing I've learned as I've got older is that rich people who go bankrupt usually have something salted away to start afresh with, so perhaps that was their case. I know they left Cranage Hall to come to Hartford.

My wages went up a couple of shillings a week, and the money was also paid to me monthly. Winnie Smith and I shared a large bedroom at the top of the house. Cook and the rest of the female staff each had their own room. The butler came in daily – he lived in King Street, Hartford. The outside staff also lived off the premises.

We had a servants' hall in which we had all our meals. The cook sat at the bottom of the table and the butler at the top. Grace was said by Mr Hollinshead before each meal.

Life was quite different. To start with, the staff all collected in the dining room 'up front', sitting on chairs placed all around the room, and waited for Mr and Mrs Carver to arrive. We had morning prayers and a hymn, then dispersed to our various departments to start work. As I have said, my duties were kitchen work only. Cook just gave me the orders for the day and said "now get on with it".

I well remember the stock pot which stood under the sink in the scullery, which held all the bones from beef or game, and the trimmings we prepared for cooking. It was all boiled up daily, and as the stock was used for soups it was replaced by water. Old bones were taken out and replaced by fresh ones – it was for ever full. I thought it stank, and I never touched any soup that was made from it for the staff.

Mr and Mrs Carver always drank a glass of hot water served each morning at 11am. The glasses were held by a silver holder so that they didn't scald their fingers.

Entertainment was nil, unless you call a temperance meeting 'entertaining'. This was held each Monday evening, when a few people came from the village to join in. After the talk, given by Mrs Carver on the evils of drinking alcohol, she would play the organ which had place of honour at the top of the dining room. At the end of the course of meetings I had to sign a form to say I would never drink alcohol, and for this I received a posh certificate. I'm afraid I broke that pledge 58 years ago, when I got married!

During my time there I remember Mr Hollinshead calling all the staff to look out of the servants' hall window to see the R101 airship which was passing over Northwich. Everyone bar me saw it. I was unlucky. I believe it crashed at a later date.

When I had my interview for my job, it was arranged that I would work for three weeks and then I would go to Ireland for two weeks, as this holiday had been arranged for some time. It was to meet and stay with my mother's Aunt Nora, who was my granddad's sister.

On my afternoon off, a day or two before I went, I took my suitcase and the clothes I needed for Mother to get ready for the journey. The cook had asked if I would drop her dirty linen off at home where her sister and daughter lived. As I rode along on my cycle, I wondered why my case was so heavy.

I arrived at the house and was asked to go in. I opened my case and handed over the parcel of 'washing'. The daughter unwrapped it on the table, and you can imagine my shock.

It was a parcel of food, sugar, tea, butter, dripping, bacon, lard, and so on. All went quiet, and pulling myself together I said "cheerio" and went on my way home.

When I got back to work that night, and Winnie and I were in bed, I told her what had happened. Winnie said: "So that's what she is up to, and she always says the housekeeper keeps giving us short rations."

You see, every morning Cook met the housekeeper to receive her daily menus and was given the fresh stores each day. Tea and sugar were issued like this, and the tea was put in an old biscuit tin. When it first came out of the store room it was three parts full, but later on it was below half, and I was always being told off for putting too much in the teapot for the brews. Anyway there must have been a bit of the devil in me because I started playing tricks on the cook. Friday was her day off and she never came up to lunch on that day. We would hear paper rustling and after a while all went quiet, and she would go to her room to get ready to go out. I would then go down to the kitchen, look around and sure enough would find the parcel hidden out of sight. I would then put it somewhere else, under cover or in a cupboard and then return to the servants' hall. When Winnie and I heard the back door close we would watch through the window, and could see a very furious lady marching off with her parcel of food.

One day I knocked the handle off a jug and Cook told me to put the jug in the cupboard, as it might come in useful one day. Now, the cupboards were big fittings all along one wall, and I could almost fit into them myself. They held dinner services, tea services, meat dishes, basins, you name it, it was in there.

One afternoon whilst tidying them up I came across the handleless jug and it was three parts full of tea. I was really mad as this was stealing our ration, so I got the staff tea tin and put nearly all of it back, and then I brewed what was left in the jug. Next I found a very large jam cover, these were used when jam making. This I stuck down and on it wrote "strawberry jam", and do you know it was still like that when I left the job after my two years were up. Winnie used to say "Yes it's still there" when I enquired about it. I think Cook must have thought it was a trap. By the way, we were able to do these things because Cook went to her room every afternoon, and the butler went home for a few hours and came back for late dinner and evening duties.

I really marvelled at myself doing these 'naughty' things because of my sheltered life at home.

The butler told us one day at the dinner table that the housekeeper had a number of false parts. Winnie and I goggled wide-eyed,

"Oh yes," said Mr Hollinshead, "it's perfectly true."

Of course we knew she was an old lady of 80 plus, she limped and puffed, and was never without her walking stick.

As usual at bedtime Winnie and I discussed the day's happenings, and we decided to find out for ourselves if the story we had been told was true.

The roof of the hall had a gully along the middle and one of our bedroom windows overlooked one in Mrs Dickenson's room, so we decided to climb out onto the roof and go along to see her get ready for bed. We climbed on to the dressing table, got out through the window and went along to wait.

We made it safely and sure enough – and this is perfectly true – she removed one by one: her false teeth, which she placed in a glass of water by her bed; her wig; a glass eye; a false breast (a piece of stiffened muslin shaped like a deep plate); and an artificial leg (which was just a peg leg, not flexible like they are today). On top of this her heart was in a bad way, so it was said.

After a while we got back into our room and we really wondered if our eyes had deceived us. We even paid another visit the next night to convince ourselves.

We were too young to understand the seriousness of such a tragedy for an elderly lady and it's a thing I've regretted doing since I've grown older and seen other cases, because she managed so well despite all these handicaps. She often went to Hartford church on Sunday morning on a three-wheel cycle. I think it must have had one pedal fixed for one legged use – I really don't know, but it's what I imagine.

Winnie and I were great friends and had many laughs together. Some nights when we went to bed there would be a treat. Between our single beds was a wooden carver chair, and we had a tray fixed across the arms. We placed a table next to it and the white cloth on it hung down to hide the seat. We used this as our hiding place and every now and again Winnie would manage to beg an apple and a drink of pop from the butler. Oh, how happy we were with the small things in life.

One of the tricks we played was on Cook on her day off. When it was time for her to come off the bus and walk down School Lane we went out to meet her and waved as she came down by Whitehall. When she came just round the bend out of sight for a minute, we would run and hide in the two big Knutsford Laundry baskets that stood in the servants' hall. As she came in the back door she always stormed past the closed baskets to the window, opened it and shouted outside to where she thought we were: "You'll stop out all night, you bad girls!"

How she never twigged where we were I will never know. She would then lock the back door and go up to the ladies maid's room for a natter, and while she was there we went up to our room. I don't know how she thought we got back into the house, but she never did fathom out how we came to be in bed when she herself came to her room. It may not seem funny as you read it but we had loads of merriment over the episodes.

I was at the Hall for two years and that was my work fin-ished as apprentice cook. I left and had a fortnight's holiday in Castlebar, County Mayo, Ireland with my Great Aunt Nora. It was she who filled me in on my granddad's childhood, up to the age of twelve years old. He ran away from home at that age and he never went back to Ireland, as I told you at the beginning of the story.

During the next eighteen months, I took up temporary work, which meant filling in between old and new staff. I got a lot of good experience and met quite a few families. In my own mind I believe that having been penned in for four years I felt like a bird let out of a cage, so I wanted a bit of freedom. Although I 'lived in' at each job I was on the move a bit more and it helped me a lot.

Amongst those jobs was one at Scullshaw Lodge, Allostock. Mrs Jaye* came to see me to ask if I would go as general help during some house parties they held throughout the racing season. They were great horse people. It was arranged for me to sleep in and give help wherever it was needed between the kitchen and upstairs, carrying Nanny's meals up. They had a baby boy and Nanny was in sole charge. She also liked to give orders. She and Cook did not get on at all well, and if Cook wanted she could be very awkward and cross swords with Nanny. Cook's son, who was about twelve years old, used to come and stay with his mother and he was always up to some mischief. One Sunday night, Cook was in one of her moods and was taking her time cooking Nanny's supper. Nanny kept ringing her bell, and she must also have complained how long she had waited. I thought I would go up to try and soothe Nanny down, and was walking towards the hall door when an object flew past my head from behind me. At the same time the hall door in front of me opened and there was Mrs Jaye. The object, a cushion, hit her right in the face. I don't know who was most surprised: all hell was let loose and she stormed back into the dining room. The boy disappeared and the dining room bell rang and rang. The parlourmaid told me that Mrs Jaye wanted to see me at once. I went in and was confronted with a very angry man. What he said to me doesn't bear to be

* Not her real name

repeated. I was blamed for the lot and given notice to be out of the house first thing next morning. He refused to listen to any explanation, and to crown it all there wasn't one of the staff who opened their mouths to defend me. They were too frightened of losing their jobs.

The next morning I was seen by Mrs Jaye and she gave me nine weeks' wages and no insurance stamps on my cards, even though it was their place to stamp my card while I was employed by them. It meant that I had to cover that out of my own pocket.

There was no such thing to my knowledge at that time as an industrial tribunal for unfair dismissal, so that was that.

A very sad thing happened a couple of months later. Mr Jaye was out riding his horse and it threw him off. He suffered, amongst other injuries, a broken neck and from then on was unable to do anything for himself. He was like that until he died a few years later.

When I look back on the incident of the cushion I can't help but smile, because Mrs Jaye stood there all bedecked with paint and powder, in evening dress and laden with jewellery, and when the cushion hit her, her face was a picture.

Strange to say everyone bar the young offspring of Mr and Mrs Jaye have long since passed away, and only I am left to remember.

After these temporary posts I took a job as 'cook general' which meant doing all cooking and the housework, bar dusting of the ornaments on the drawing room mantelpiece. I was not trusted with this job in case I broke any! The main laundry went out. This was for Mr and Mrs Troon* in Walnut Lane, Hartford. Again I was a resident with half a day off per week. On the whole things were not at all bad here, although other than a couple of families down that road the rest were rather toffee-nosed, even the ones I worked for. One instance sticks in my mind. One Sunday afternoon Mr Troon asked if I would go to post a letter at

* Not their real name

Rutter's postbox. Being glad of the fresh air I willingly said "yes". It was a lovely day so I took off my cap and small apron and set off with my plain black frock and no coat. On my return I was met at the gate by Mr Troon, who said: "If you knew how awful you looked without your uniform, you'd never go out without it."

No, I wasn't dreaming, those words were actually said to me. I was so stunned that I reacted in rather an odd way for me. I went inside, picked up my cap and put it in the stove to burn. I vowed would never wear one again.

I put his manner down to sheer ignorance. What an example of education, at Marlborough House no less! I was taught better at home at Shipbrook.

Anyway, things and work carried on. Our postman was Mr Philip Dickens from Leftwich Green. He was a kindly man, very cheerful and always whistling on his rounds. I was usually cleaning the doorsteps when he came and would have a chat. It turned out that he had delivered the post to Thorn Farm as a young boy and had known my mother. It was he who told me such a lot about her, how hard she had to work and how when she was suffering all that trouble with her face, he told me, often she would be walking about in the farmyard in the early morning, having been up most the night in pain. Oh yes, he told me a lot, did Philip, as we called him. Thank you Philip.

One day Mrs Troon asked me if I would like a pair of silk stockings, as she was unable to wear them because there was a small ladder at the back. Now, to own a pair of silk stockings in those days was a dream – we wore ones made from unglamorous lisle – so ladder or not I said "thank you".

I used my sewing skills and mended the short ladder, and to my amazement when I was wearing them once Mrs Troon asked me if those were the stockings she had given me. I replied "yes", and her answer to that was: "Had I known you could do a repair like that I would have got you to mend them for me."

Yes, that was generosity in those days – give with one hand and take away with the other.

Eventually Mrs Troon became an expectant mother. As time went on she got rather irritable, and was inclined to take her temper out on me. Nothing seemed to be right but I put up with it, and eventually the baby arrived.

A few weeks before this event I had been asked if I would go to work daily, instead of sleeping in. I agreed to this arrangement because my room was needed for a nanny! I did say that as it meant me cycling from Shipbrook I would arrive and start work at 7.30am to give me time to get there. It meant that the only job I couldn't fit in before breakfast was to brush the stairs down and clean and dust the hall. I was told not to worry, it was all right.

These arrangements went on fine for a long time, but then I was told to try and do it all as before so that the hall and stairs were cleaned before breakfast. I tried but it was no good.

Things became a bit edgy and I began to get fed up with their complaints, so one morning as I was being told off about it, I turned round and asked Mrs Troon to take my notice. After I had cooled down I told her that I would stay until she got fixed up with a replacement, for which she was very grateful. She even said "sorry" for going off the handle.

I was tidying up the linen cupboard when Mr Troon came home for lunch, and after a talk with Madam he came to me and said: "You can take your notice now, and don't come in on Monday morning."

"All right," I said, "thank you."

I got my wages up to Sunday. Had I gone to work on Monday that would have meant them putting an insurance stamp on my card. I had to see to that myself. Today it would be called unfair dismissal.

I was at home for about three weeks and then Mrs Troon got in touch with me, saying she would like me to go and see her about to taking up my post again. It seems that the replacement had cleared off while they were at the pictures, leaving them with the washing up from late dinner.

I went for the interview and listened to why I was expected to go back after my quick dismissal.

"We really have missed you. We got on so well and you ran the cooking and the work to perfect timing," she said. I was even told that if I did go back I could also have any of her clothes she discarded, instead of giving them to her cousin as before – some deal! Anyway, I said if I did go back I would like 2/6d per week extra, which would bring my wages up to 17/6d per week. She agreed, but as I had no intention of going back there again I just said: "You'll hear from me."

The first phone box I came to, I rang and said I was sorry, but it wasn't for me.

About a week later I met a friend, Louie Crimes, who also worked in Walnut Lane. She said: "Oh, by the way, Nellie, I've got some news for you. Mrs So & So (her boss) gave a tea party the other day and while I was waiting on I heard Mrs Troon, who was one of the guests, tell the other five visitors that she had thought about asking you back to work for her, but it was out of the question as you had demanded £1 per week."

You can imagine my reaction to that. The next day I got on my bike and called on each person who had been to the tea party.

I explained what had been said at my interview and told them that I had no intention of going back after the way Mr Troon had spoken to me on the day I gave my notice in.

I only saw Mr and Mrs C Marsh, one of those families from Walnut Lane again, and they were friends to me until they left the district many years later. Sadly they have now passed away. The children's nanny, Jean Sinclair from Rhynie, Aberdeenshire, and I have remained friends to this day. She used to spend her time off at my home and was like a sister.

CHAPTER SEVEN

Lady's Companion/Help

My father, in his old age

I heard about my next job from the insurance man who used to call for the premiums for Pearl. He told me there was a situation going in Hale as parlour-maid where his cousin worked, for a Mr and Miss Leaf who were brother and sister. An interview was arranged for me and I was successful in getting the job.

I had a shock when it came to cleaning utensils, for they had nothing modern. There was just a hand brush and dust-pan for all the carpets, and it was back to the old washbasins on a marble washstand, and solid oak furniture which was all joiner-made and had been in the family for years. I don't know Mr Walter's age, but Miss Rose Leaf was in her late 80s at that time, around 1935-36. I know there was the scandal about the Prince of Wales and Mrs Simpson going on and he gave up the throne. I remember, I was going along Hale Road to catch the train on my afternoon off, when I heard the abdication announced as I passed a shop.

The train I travelled on for my afternoons off was called 'The Dripping Train'. This name went on for many years because the cooks came from the Northwich district and worked around Altrincham, Sale, Hale, and so forth. They would bring home the dripping left from all the big beef joints that they were allowed to dispose of, hence the name of the train.

There were only two indoor staff, Cook and myself. Mr Smith, almost as ancient as the Leafs, was the gardener, and he was a wonderful man. I don't know how he managed all that work including a tennis court, for the garden was huge.

After a few months Cook left and a couple more followed. They never settled, I think owing to the old fashioned range and primus oil stove used for cooking. In the end I was left to do the lot. A couple of years passed and I had to go into the Manchester Ear, Nose and Throat Hospital for an operation on my throat. I never went back. When I recovered from my operation I worked in Davenham for a widow, Mrs Manley*. She lived in a big house called Merebank House, sadly now demolished to make room for a housing estate which took the name Merebank, and I believe the ground and surrounding fields are now covered with houses and bungalows. It is so sad to see green fields disappearing for ever.

I think it was in 1937-8 that I got a chill that led to chest trouble and high temperatures, and the doctor paid a number of visits daily for four days, then periodically until I began to show signs of improvement. I also had visits each evening for a week from the district nurse who took my temperature. Eventually I recovered, but my doctor was not satisfied that my chest was quite right. I was sent to see a

* Not her real name

64

specialist and he asked me if I would be willing to go to Market Drayton Sanatorium in Shropshire to have some special tests and three months' rest in the open air.

I told my parents. It was discussed and decided that I should go. You see at that time there was a common disease called consumption (tuberculosis), and many people died from it, so my medics wanted to make sure that I had none of the symptoms.

When I arrived there, it was out in the wilds and such a cold place – that apparently was part of the treatment. Our accommodation was an open-sided, two-bed bedroom so that you got wind, rain, snow or whatever came along. Another girl arrived at the same time as me and we shared one of the 'cells', as we called them. Her name was Vera and we became great friends, and still are to this day sixty-odd years later.

My parents could not afford to come very often as it meant hiring a taxi, for there was no public transport. My dad and Uncle Walter cycled to see me a few times, but other than that I had no one. Vera's mother was wonderfully good to me. She came every week and would bring each of us lovely salads and sweets for our Sunday tea. I was never left out. I became very fond of Mrs Clegg, who treated me like her own daughter up to the day she died.

I had a number of tests and the last one meant poppy oil being injected via the throat. If it showed up on the screen as having gone through certain organs in the chest, it meant I was clear of any TB infection. I remember hearing the specialist saying "Thank God, that is another one all right", and then I passed out. I woke up in my bed with a nurse by my side. She said: "Well, my dear, you'll be off home tomorrow."

I was so happy to be going home, but also sad that there were so many people there who would never go home. My dear friend Vera had to stay in over a year because she needed treatment. I'm happy to say she recovered fully and still lives a few miles from me.

Vera never married and her love and time were taken up

with her sisters and their families. My children also had some very happy holidays and outings with her. We were taken on visits to the lovely country houses such as Gawsworth Hall and Capesthorne Hall, and we also spent weekends at her house. These were pleasures we would never have had because we had no transport of our own.

Now my daughters are grown up and have families of their own, but they never forget Aunty Vera. I had only been home from hospital about two weeks and a family friend, the district nurse who had been at my birth, popped in and asked me to go round to see her husband's Aunt Louie, who was staying with them for a while. It appears that she had lost her two daughters, at 23 and 25 years old, and her husband had died while playing golf. All this tragedy had taken place in two years. She was very low in spirits and was looking for a companion/help to live with her and to be company.

I went round, and over a cup of tea we chatted and discussed the situation. We took to each other straight away and it was arranged that I would go back with her on the Monday to Chester Road, Hartford.

The only family she had left was her son who lived at Whitegate. He called on Saturdays but they seemed to argue quite a bit over money, so I always left them together.

She and I got on very well and I became fond of her. I never had days off but used to often walk home to Davenham in an afternoon, have a cup of tea and a chat, and then head back for teatime. Often on these trips I would take a neighbour's two little boys, Sandy and Graham Guthrie, in the pram with me. It was great company for me and gave Mrs Guthrie a break. A couple of times Mrs Barlow and Rhona who lived next door took us by car to Chester, and we would have afternoon tea in a huge store. I think it was Browns of Chester.

Other times Mrs Sims and I would do a bit of gardening. I never went out at night and our entertainment was reading, listening to the wireless and chatting. I did such things as embroidery and sewing to pass the time. I wonder how many girls of 24-25 years old would do that today. Often I've been asked how I went on for boyfriends in my young days. I hardly met any and as you have learned by my story there was no chance to go dancing and mix, but I don't regret any of this – it was my lot and I took it for granted.

I remember sitting in the kitchen and heard on the wireless that war had been declared. Mrs Sims and I fixed a cosy shelter under the stairs in case any bombs were dropped and carried on as usual. We were issued with gas masks and always had them handy.

I found it very hard to cope on the small wage I received each week, and after I'd been there nearly two years I asked Mrs Sims if she could raise my money by 2/6 per week. I was taken aback by her reaction – I thought she was going to have some sort of an attack. She went mad and said: "You ask me for more money, when I took you in when no one else would have you. I wasn't frightened of catching anything from you."

I was absolutely dumbfounded. What of my feelings? I was sleeping in the bed where her poor daughter had died from that terrible consumption.

When I could speak I said to her: "I'm sorry, but I was *asked* to come and work for you! And in any case I never had anything for you to catch, so you have nothing to worry about. Keep your money and look for another companion, because there's no way can I stay with you now."

After two weeks I left and went to the ICI Wallerscote soda ash bagging plant on war work.

I spoke to my doctor and told him what had happened. He said it was better to get away from Mrs Sims. I also wrote to Mr Edwards, the specialist at Market Drayton, and he was most kind. He sent me a signed certificate saying I had never had tuberculosis and he wished all the patients he saw in his hospital could get the same results that I'd had. He also offered me a nursing job in his hospital. I would have loved that but it was such a difficult place to get to and too far away. I thanked him very much.

My life changed at ICI. My working hours were from 7.30am to 5pm, then it was home on the bus, have a bath and change, cook the meal and afterwards I had a whole evening to myself.

September came in and Dad, Uncle Walter and my sister Joyce were taking the odd Sunday night bike trips as we had done some years before. They decided to go out one Sunday evening as the weather was good. I was going to stay in but my mother said: "Oh no, you're not going to sit there all night moping, get off with them for a run and get some fresh air."

We took the Sandbach run and did as before. First stop was the Military Arms and then on to the Duke of Portland at Lach Dennis. By this time Joyce and I felt brave enough to go inside for our lemonade and had a nice chat with Mrs Edwards, our friend the landlady. After a while a number of young airmen came in and Mrs Edwards said: "These are the lads from the local air station."

Joyce and I said "Hello" and that was all the conversation we had. They did talk to Dad and Uncle Walter. A couple of them said goodnight to us as we left and added: "We'll see you again some time."

A couple of nights later Joyce and I went for a ride round hoping to see some of the planes on the airfield, but we saw nothing – there wasn't a living soul about. We decided to return via Middlewich. As we came towards the village of Byley we passed two airmen and they called out "Hello" to us. One of them said: "Aren't you the girls we saw in the Duke's?"

We got off our bikes for a word and ended up walking all the way to Middlewich just wandering and chatting. The one I talked to told me his name was "Ralph" and his home town, and I learned all about his life before he joined up. I told him my story and he asked me for my address.

We eventually arrived at Middlewich and stood chatting on the station bridge. To me all this was a new experience. Here I was, 26 years old, and this was the first time in my life that I had held such a pleasant, interesting conversation with a young man.

As we stood there we heard the sounds of a German plane probably on its way to Warrington or Liverpool, so the boys said it would be better if we made our way home, telling us to lie down in the ditch at the side of the road if there was sign of a bombing.

Just before we said goodnight, Ralph said to me: "I'll marry you one day."

I thought that was amusing and laughed. I never dreamt what the outcome would be.

We had an uneventful journey home. A few days later I received a letter from Ralph asking me to meet him again. I was a bit dubious but thought, "Well, there was no nonsense about him, I'll be all right," so it was arranged by letter that he would come to Davenham.

He ended up visiting my home for a meal a week or two later and we got on like a house on fire. He didn't get much food at his billet and loved my mother's home cooking, especially the rabbit and apple pies.

After five months the boys were warned of a move abroad and Ralph said he

Me around the time of our wedding

69

Ralph Osborne

would like us to get married, as we had by that time become so close and in love. He had a word with my mother and father, who had both become very fond of him.

We arranged for our wedding to be held on April 12, 1941 at Davenham church. It was just ten days after my 27th birthday and happened to be Easter Saturday. I had asked Miss Mann our boss at ICI if I could have the following Tuesday off, as I was going to Northampton for a couple of days. She said "no" as too many other people were having time off, and I told her that I would not be in on Tuesday. She said if I did that I would get the sack and be made an example of.

The wedding was lovely and we went off to stay with Ralph's parents for a couple of days. On my return to work on the Wednesday morning I was sent for by Miss Mann, who did give me a week's notice. It was the best thing that could have happened because the chemicals I worked with did not suit my skin, so I was glad to get away. You see, there was no way you could leave war work unless there was some special reason.

The sun seemed to shine on Ralph and me. The move abroad didn't come and for two years we had a wonderful time. He worked shifts at the wireless station, way out in the fields at Boots Green near to

Aunt Sally (Sarah Whalley) and Dad (her brother-in-law) on our wedding day.

Goostrey, and I took on the task of night nurse to a few people who would not get better. They were looked after and nursed at home by their families, for there were no nursing homes like today. These were usually elderly mums or grannies. Miss James did the day nursing and I did the nights. I loved that job. I had breaks between each one so it meant I had a lot of spare time. I used to ride to work with Ralph and meet him at the end of his shift.

During the mushroom season I would roam across the fields on my journeys and gather loads of mushrooms, then there were the blackberries. I knew all the good places to go, and the basket on the front of my bike was always full of something. One day on my way down Crowders Lane I saw a rabbit cross the road and following it was a stoat. There was a cry and there just in the field was the rabbit. I climbed over the fence and got the dead rabbit, and finally rode home with the next day's dinner in my basket.

Another day I noticed something rather strange in an old tree stump in the hedge. On investigation I discovered thirteen hen's eggs. It must have been a hen 'laying away' (as it was called) because there no farms close by. Into my basket they went and my first job on arriving home was to get a bowl of water to test the eggs. They were all perfect so it meant extra rations again. Everything helped in those days.

71

I collected a fresh egg for our daily breakfast from the same spot for some weeks.

We still waited for the move abroad and the order came almost two years to the day after we had first expected it. We were staying in Northampton with Ralph's mum and dad when we got word that Ralph had to report to his base in Formby. We came back to Davenham and while Ralph was getting all his stuff together, I rode to Boots Green to see the other boys to find out what was happening, and to collect a few things that he kept at the station.

To my astonishment the other five boys had gone and they had been replaced. I went home, we had a meal and walked to Hartford station to catch the next train to Liverpool. What a journey! We had Ralph's bike with us, but it had a flat tyre. It was Government property and as Ralph had signed for it with his kit, he said everything had to be returned to base.

It was late when we arrived in Liverpool and very dark. We crossed the city to get a train to Formby, bike and all. When we arrived we were too late to report at the office and were told to come back at 9am the next day. Now where were we to go? I had a friend who had been living in Freshfield, but we hadn't been in touch for some time. Anyway, we decided to find out and see if she would put up with us for the night. We were lucky, they were just going to bed. Cissie and Bob made us very welcome, and as her home was a billet for servicemen, after some refreshment we went into the sitting room and spent the night sleeping in two armchairs. We were most grateful, as we both had a good sleep after such a long tiring day.

I stayed with Cissie the next day while Ralph went to sign in and get his orders. He came back after lunch and said we had to go to Blackpool, where he would be fitted out with tropical kit and put in a billet until he was shipped off.

Away we went again and eventually arrived very late. We got a taxi and went looking for lodgings for the night. It seemed hopeless. You see, not only were all these troops there, as it was the main stepping-off base, there was also a big conference on and all the boarding houses seemed to be booked up.

It was over an hour before the driver spotted a tiny chink of light through a curtain which was not properly drawn, so he pulled up. It was on Albert Road and on enquiring we were lucky. The gentleman said: "We have just a small room at the top of the stairs."

The spotless white sheets and the cleanliness of the place! I should say we fell into bed, we were so tired. I was wakened by a terrible itching all over my body, and found I was covered with big red blotches. I woke Ralph and told him. He said: "I'm all right – you must be allergic to something."

Anyway, when he reported the next morning to base he was fitted out and given an address where he would stay until sent abroad. His landlady told him that I could stay with him as she had a single room. Some of her lads had been shipped off, as the men never had any warning of the move. They reported each morning at the base and if it was their turn they just disappeared. You didn't know where they were until you had a letter; mine came from North Africa after two or three weeks.

We were in that house just over a week and I had the same trouble in that bed as in the first. When I told Mrs Clegg, Vera's mother, who then lived in Bispham, she said: "Bring all the clothes you are not wearing and I will stove them for you. I'm afraid you've hit the dreaded 'bugs'". She explained that the foreign troops had brought them in and Blackpool was infested with them.

By the following lunchtime I think I had bought all the Keatings Powder in Blackpool. I smothered our bed in it and those of the other servicemen. That was easy because I helped to make the beds and tidy the rooms as a thanks for being allowed to stay with Ralph.

On the Saturday Ralph did not come back from base and I

had no message as to why. The landlady told me that I would have to wait until he reached his post abroad. As I said earlier, that is what happened.

Mrs Clegg had told me to let her know when Ralph went. She wanted me to go and spend two weeks at their house in Bispham before going to Northampton, where I was to start as a probationer at St Andrew's Private Mental Hospital. I had got the post through my mother-in-law who also worked there.

Vera and I were very happy to have time together, for we had a lot to talk about. On Sunday morning we took her dog, Sandy, for a walk along the beach, which was covered with big wire barriers and was very restricted for space. We stood together looking out to sea and there wasn't even a small boat or another soul about. I said to Vera: "I wonder where Ralph is now?"

She said: "No one knows. Everything is kept secret because of enemy 'U' boats".

We stood meditating and all of a sudden I gave a shout. I'd felt something quite warm trickle down my ankle. I startled Vera. I looked down at my leg and there was a little white dog who had his leg cocked and was spending a penny against me. I dare say he had a scent of Sandy, I can't think of any other explanation. Vera told me to take it as an omen of good luck that Ralph would come home. We've often laughed about it.

CHAPTER EIGHT
Wife and Nurse

Ralph, Diana, me and Veronica

alph was away a good three years. He spent his time in North Africa and Italy, then went to Austria. I was told all this when he came home because all letters were censored and we never knew where they came from.

I spent those three years at St Andrew's Hospital, part of which was taken over by the Government for members of the Forces to be treated for such things as breakdowns and other mental disturbances. I nursed many officers and other ranks of the women's Forces and met some wonderful people.

One night when I was on duty I met Sarah Churchill, Sir Winston's daughter. She was an ambulance driver and brought a patient in. I gave her a cup of tea and had a lovely

chat with her. She was glad of the
break before she returned to her
base.

While nursing there I can say
what satisfaction I got. It was
wonderful to see a smile after the
great torment the patients were
suffering when they came in.

I have a memory of a beautiful
young mother of two children, a
great Lord's daughter. She had
been an ambulance driver during
the London Blitz. She had
worked herself to a complete
standstill mentally and I'm
afraid all our treatment failed to
help. She was taken back to her
ancestral home in Ireland with
two nurses in charge. I often
think of her and wonder what
happened to her husband, who
was a doctor, and those two lovely
children.

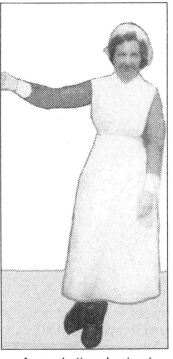

*A very battered cut-out
snapshot of me as a nurse
at St Andrew's*

We carry on in our lives and how many of us say "thank
you" to such wonderful people who did war work like that?
What appreciation did they get at the end of the day? I will
remember them to my dying day, as I do all the servicemen
and women. God bless them all.

What I learned in those three years has stood me in good
stead ever since and has helped me to cope with many situ-
ations that I have since come across during my lifetime.

I worked shifts to start with and worked so many days at
different times. It meant I got three days off together at the
end of each four weeks, which enabled me to go back home
to Davenham for a weekend.

The last year I worked all night duty, often twelve hours at a time, and sometimes we were not relieved to have a drink or a break. Six months of this I spent on the block for suicidal patients, working five nights on and two off. This took a toll on my health because by this time I had rented a flat and got a home of my own together, for when Ralph returned from abroad.

It was the upstairs of a house and shop, and the woman who owned it lived downstairs on the two lower floors. A month or two after I had moved in and had decorated it and settled down, there was an influx of Londoners who moved into the district to get away from the bombing and they were paying very big money for accommodation. This appeared to be a good opportunity for Mrs Shakely, my landlady. From then on my life was different.

The tricks that woman played on me to get me out were unbelievable. Being on nights at the hospital, working twelve hour shifts, meant me having to get as much sleep as I could. If I slept during the mornings her daughter was sent to practise piano lessons in her dinner hour from school. If I tried to sleep in the afternoons the piano practising happened after school, and I got very nasty remarks and complaints. I began to dread being off duty. I tried everywhere to get other accommodation but it was impossible and in the end my health suffered.

One weekend, during my three days off, our family doctor paid a visit to my mother, and as we were talking I asked him for a tonic to buck me up. After a lot of questions I ended up being off work for three months with a breakdown. The doctor forbade me to go back to Northampton until he said otherwise. He got in touch with Matron and told her that I was in no fit state to carry on nursing at that time.

I would not like to go through all that again.

I did go back to pay my flat rent for a few weeks in advance, to secure my home. I went through a very bad stage and it didn't help that I was worrying what Ralph's position was abroad and how he was faring. Anyway, I got on well and instead of going on the wards, Matron gave me the job of telephonist on the hospital switchboard. I enjoyed the work but missed the patients very much.

My first year's wages when I started working at St Andrews were £4.19.8 per month, and the second year they went up to £5.15.4. When I took the flat I paid 25/- per week rent, on top of this I had to pay for my coal for heating and so much for gas and electricity. All this made a big hole in my allowance from Ralph. Also there were food and clothes to buy. My motto was 'make do and mend'.

I bought my furniture for so much a week from Mr Parkinson who sold new and second-hand furniture. I did get the best I could for my money. My pantry was an alcove with shelves made from two double orange boxes painted white. A long curtain hanging from a wire was the door and I was very proud of all this.

When Ralph was demobbed in November 1945 he went back to his old job at Mansfield's shoe factory. We still lived over the shop and a few months later I discovered I was pregnant.

One evening while I was at work there was an accident. After a film had been on for the patients upstairs a young boy was lowering the equipment over the balcony. The rail he was leaning over gave way and he fell down to the ground, landing underneath the window where I sat at the stitchboard. I heard the noise and screams and thought a patient had jumped from the window above.

It gave me a great shock. I am pleased to say his injuries were just a broken leg and wrist – everyone expected far worse because it was such a long drop.

Sadly, I took a toll myself and lost my baby.

We lived at the flat for about another six months until I heard of another one and was lucky, or so I thought, to get it.

A young couple, Mr and Mrs Bosley, had rented a house and lived on the ground floor. They rented me the first floor with a shared bathroom. This again I got for 25/- per week plus bills, as before.

I carried on with my job and a year later I was pregnant again. We had a baby girl, Veronica, on January 22, 1947, nearly six years after we were married. I will never forget that time, it was the great freeze of 1947. Even the bedpans were frozen – what great memories!

Veronica is now 52 years old. When I came out of hospital the fun started. The landlady and her husband had always gone to bed at 9.30pm and we had been expected to do the same, but with a baby things were different. I hardly dared walk about, and as for the baby it was a crime for her to cry. I tried to get a council house but was told half a house was enough, and to give the landlady as good as I got. Not being an aggressive sort, I couldn't do that.

In the end my mum and dad told us to move to their house, and this we did. Ralph got a job at ICI Lostock and we started to look for our own house. After a few months we heard that Davenham Conservative Club (now the Players' theatre) required a new stewardess, so I applied and was lucky. It wasn't very big accommodation, but two bedrooms, a small living room and kitchen to me was heaven – however, I still kept trying for a council house. When we first came back to Davenham I went to see Mr Warburton, a council man who lived in Green Lane House. I explained my situation and asked if he could help me to get a council house. His answer was: "Your sister has got one, one in the family is enough."

So much for six years of service to your country!

Since coming back I had taken cleaning jobs at the grand wage of 1/3d an hour, later I got 2/6d per hour but it was a case of take it or leave it. Every bit added up to enable us to save a little towards a proper home for when the time came.

My mother helped me by looking after Veronica. She was four years old when our second daughter Diana was born on February 9, 1951, and when Diana was 18 months old we learned that we had been allocated a council house. We moved into 4 Charles Avenue, Davenham on the day Veronica started school. That was in May 1952 and we are still there in 1999 as I sit here writing my story.

We've had our ups and downs but we have been, and still are, very happy and thank God every day for our blessings.

I kept my three-hour morning jobs to make ends meet, as Ralph's wages were just over £4 per week. The story I am telling applies to many couples who were in the same boat – we were forced to work for a pittance to enable us to survive. I'm amazed at the people who pretend they led a different kind of life. The true honest friends I've got are proud like me, of the way we surmounted all the obstacles and unhappy times we had to survive.

Some of the people I worked for treated me like muck, as we used to say. Of course there were also the lovely ones who treated me as a human being and it was a pleasure to work for them. I am still in touch with one lady, now a widow, and we talk over old times when we get the chance. So many have passed from this world but memories remain for me, both good and bad.

One thing has always amazed me: we working girls always had to supply two or three references about our character and honesty, but you never got to ask the would-be employers for theirs. Now, this should work both ways. We often read in the papers where a maid, nursemaid or whatever has had their character blackened, that they were this and that and the other, but there's never a word about their employer. Both sides should be heard.

I also feel disgusted and sickened when I read today of the excuses that are made to get thousands of pounds' worth of compensation. I know one or two cases are genuine but usually it's any excuse to get their hands on easy money. These people should have faced what we had to endure. There was no fairness, and another thing, we didn't turn to drugs, we didn't know such things existed. I have no sympathy at all for drug addicts. There are plenty of voluntary, worthwhile jobs to do to get out of a rut. I say: "Just think of others for a change, you will feel all the better for it."

I can look back at all the things that happened to me and often see the funny side, because I can now say each cloud had a silver lining. Something good came out of most of these incidents, even Mrs Sims' nasty remark about my health caused me to leave, and look what happened.

Life went on. The girls went off to school, Ralph changed his job and went to work for Octel at Plumley, and we settled down.

CHAPTER NINE

'Mam Osborne'

Me during my years as a foster-mother

I n about 1963 the council asked householders if they could help by accommodating one or two children while a mother was in hospital, or because the family could not manage for other reasons. It was just for short term visits. After discussing it with Veronica and Diana we decided to have a go, and as a family with a good record we were chosen.

Veronica was off school after a severe illness and we felt it would help her if she had another interest.

At first we had Pamela for six weeks, and she was about five years old. She settled down well and was very happy with us. We were never told why these children had to be looked after, they just came and went. A few months went by before we were asked to take another child. She was about nine years old and oh, how she loved to help. Running errands was her favourite thing, she seemed to love being wanted. I have often thought about her over the years. She stayed about three weeks with us, and then came Olive who was ten or eleven years old and stayed for a year. She started going to Hartford Secondary School while she was with us.

Each child needed a different understanding and love was most essential. I remember the nine year old: we knew for about a week that she would be going home and it was just before Christmas. One day my niece, who was visiting us to play with the girls, came to me. She said: "Aunt Nell, did you know that Christine will only have a butty for her Christmas dinner?"

"Nonsense!" I said.

"Oh no," she answered, "she says her mother won't cook."

Ralph and I talked it over and put a special Christmas party on for her, and my word, did she enjoy herself. We and the girls all gave her presents and she had a lovely time – at least she had a good Christmas dinner.

All was back to normal for quite a while and then we were asked if we would take a little girl of four and a half years old until a permanent home could be found, as she was a ward of court and would not be returning to her own home again. If we could cope it would be what the Social Services called 'long term'. They explained that we would be family number five, including one family who had tried twice to cope and had given up on her. After great discussions we decided to take her on. We had her for a day, then a weekend, and eventually she came to stay. Apparently people said they found her too difficult to cope with.

We fell in love with this child, Sharon*, she was so affectionate. I won't go into details, but after a while as she got a bit older I realised things were not as they should be. I got

*Not her real name

in touch with my doctor and explained my anxiety, and he agreed that it must be discussed with the Social Services. This I did and I asked to see a child specialist. After a lot of humming and ha'ing I got to see one.

After the interview he talked to me. He was very surprised that the council had not told me even a little about the child's health and background and explained why the poor girl had been moved from one place to another. He read me her case history and I learned that she had inherited her parents' problems. He said I had done the right thing to seek help and he in turn gave me some very good advice which enabled me to cope much better.

We still carried on and after about four years a new law came out that all fostered children should be told what family they had, and we understood that they should meet each other at least three or four times a year.

We discovered that Sharon had a sister Tanya* who had lived on the Wirral since they had been removed from their real parents, and breaking the news was quite an ordeal. It had to be explained very carefully because children don't understand as we older people do.

All seemed well and both families were introduced and the girls met. Tanya had been with her 'mum and dad', as she called them, had accepted them almost from the beginning, and their own son and daughter were like her family.

All went well for a few months and all seemed fine on the surface. But on Tanya's ninth birthday her party was to have 'tea with Mummy', and she was told that her parents, whom she understood were dead, were actually alive. Before she was nine and a half years old we were asked by the council if we would have her to stay for a week or two, while her family moved down to London and settled into a new home, as her father had lost his job and it meant them each staying with their respective parents until they finally got fixed up.

*Not her real name

We thought it would be nice for the two sisters to get to know each other really well. Tanya had been with that family from two years old, I understood. Mrs Romark* even sent her own little bed so that it would 'comfort her'.

To this day I believe Social Services knew what was going on. We had a dreadful time with Tanya, God knows what sort of childhood she'd had. The poor thing didn't even know how to play with other children. I kept her occupied with all sorts of things, for my home was full of kiddies from around, and then came the blow. Mrs Romark wrote me a letter through the Social Services to tell me they were not going to have Tanya back, and believe it or not it was left for me to tell that child the truth. My heart ached for her, she was inconsolable. Both Ralph and I tried and tried but she was devastated. In the end I had to give her the letter I had received from Mrs Romark, and in time it sank in.

A very big question arose out of all this. Tanya was almost ten years old now and to have had all that trauma in the last twelve months, was terrible. She was left with no home to go to, and when I asked the social worker what the situation was, he said that unless a home could be found with a family she would have to be put in a children's home. This to us was out of the question. Ralph and I talked and talked about how we could help that child. We said that at least she had been with us for a while, was used to the girls and someone had to help who understood what she had gone through.

In the end we asked the council to consider us as the foster parents who would take over. We were accepted at once. This is where I must praise my own family – Ralph, Veronica and Diana – because without their help and the way they shared with the ups and downs I'm sure it could not have been done.

I remember clearly, a woman said to me one day: "Oh, well, you get paid for having them."

Believe me, the money, which was a pittance in those days,

*Not her real name

was never the issue. My own thoughts on looking after these children was always of my own mother and how different it would have been for her to have had a loving home, instead of being thrown into the workhouse. No, it was my family who sacrificed for those children and gave them our love.

A year or two later I was approached by the council, who had a problem. They were looking for a suitable family to give a home to Rosemary*, a young girl. The circumstances meant it was urgent. I said we would help if we could, but four girls were really enough to cope with. They explained that was the reason I had been chosen, as they wanted her to be with young people.

"By the way," I asked, "how old is this child?" and the answer was sixteen years old.

"In that case," I said, "you had better ask her if she would like to come, because there's no way can you just place her anywhere."

I said to bring her along for a cup of tea and let her meet the family, and she could then decide if it was what she would like.

They came when the girls were back from school and we had told my four about all this so they knew what to expect. All went well and really it was as if they had always known each other.

Eventually Rosemary and the Social Worker left and I had said: "Think it over well and make your mind up yourself. If you decide to come to us you will be made most welcome, and we will do all we can to make you happy. Let us know what you decide."

It was barely two hours and I was told that she would love to come. She moved in straight away. I bought bunk beds and the rooms had to be shared, but all went quite well. I decided to let her bring a couple of personal items with her, a wardrobe, sewing machine and a number of smaller items. She had to dispose of her home owing to a family death, and

*Not her real name

Pictured on our golden wedding anniversary in 1991.

I thought it would bring her some comfort to have a bit of the old place with her.

My wonderful reward to Ralph and the family is that we are still Mum, Dad and sisters to our children who were first 'borrowed'. God is good. In 35 years we've had a big family.

They are all married now and all have wonderful children who in turn, are all doing well as they grow up. They have all been brought up in the same way I was brought up – it is a lesson that seems to have been handed down and it has paid off. I am a very lucky woman.

Veronica, my eldest daughter, is herself now a granny, and we are great-grandparents for the first time. Mark was one year old on 15.5.99.

My last daughter, Rosemary, who had been left alone when the last member of the foster family that she had been with for some years had died, knew her real father was living and she found out his whereabouts and got in touch with him. I'm so glad they were reunited and became very close. They saw each other often and spent happy times together, and he was able to enjoy the company of his grandchildren. Sadly he passed away about two years ago.

About four years ago I heard by chance that Olive, my twelve-month visitor, had told someone I knew that she had lived in Davenham with 'Mam Osborne', and that they were the happiest days she"d had. I felt proud that a child had remembered after 39 years and it showed that at least we had helped her in some way.

Now time has gone on and I would like to tell you what happened in April 1999. It was my 85th birthday on April 2, our 58th wedding anniversary on April 12 and on April 15 I went round to see my friend, Ann Kettle, who had recently lost her dear husband. I got to the gate as the bus pulled up beside me. My sister got off and behind her came a young woman. She said: "Hello, Mam – you don't know me, do you?"

I said: "I'm sorry, but I have no idea who you are."

"I'm Olive, Mam, and I've come to see you."

Her arms went round my neck and I was hugged so tight. We went back home and the same thing happened with Ralph. He asked her why we'd never had a visit before and she explained everything. How she had gone back to her mother, how her dad died and how her mother's health wasn't good – also how she herself had all sorts of things wrong. The poor girl had wires attached to different parts of her body and she also wore big irons up her legs, but that day she said she was having a rest from them.

She was now married very happily and her husband was the driver of the small bus. She said: "We have no children because of my health and it wouldn't be fair to them."

We admired her for this. She spoke a lot about the time she spent with us.

She said: "Do you remember, Mam? I wasn't an easy child to deal with but you were patient and helped me."

She spoke lovingly of my daughters and remembered many things.

Olive explained that while she was at the secondary school at Hartford she had been helped with her education and it was discovered that she was dyslexic. They worked hard with her and she made great progress and passed her exams. To me, all this and seeing her after 39 years, was a wonderful ending to my anniversary, and it has made my family so happy to think that Olive made the grade like all the others.

I will now go back to my work days. As the different families for whom I worked regular three hours left the district, I had more time to myself and one morning Mr Palin, the headmaster from the village school, got in touch with me. They were desperate for a 'dinner lady', as they were called then, and asked if I could possibly help out for a few weeks. I was delighted – and believe it or not I was there for almost 20 years. What a happy time those years were. It was a pleasure to go to work for those two and a half hours each day.

Mr Palin was the kindest, most understanding man I've had the pleasure of working for, and the other dinner staff – Molly, Marion and Margaret ('inside ladies'), Marjorie and Doreen ('outside ladies') – were what I call the most perfect workmates. Thank you, girls, for your friendship.

I loved the children. One of the dinner tables was just the other side of the service hatch and I played a little game with the young ones on it. I used to say: "There will be a star on my kitchen wall for the first one to eat all their dinner."

It worked ten out of ten times because they all had clean plates!

I was presented with a lovely set of suitcases when I retired at 65 years of age, and it was a very sad day for me.

Two years went by. Ralph retired from Octel, and a couple of weeks later I went into hospital for an operation. I was away three weeks and Ralph kept the house for the first time. He was a master cook of stews, and they were lovely. Anyway, he coped.

When I came home we booked a coach trip to Woolacombe

in Devon for a week as a treat, and it was very nice. We went on these tours for about four years and after that decided home was best.

My family have since used my presentation suitcases to go to many places and I really don't know who has them now.

A wonderful interest I've had for about 45 years is being a member of the Royal British Legion along with Ralph. I've held various positions on committees, and was for a good many years a committee member of the Women's Section, whose motto is "Service not Self".

I became the welfare officer, and as I said earlier in my story the knowledge I gathered during my nursing days held me in good stead for that job. I was in my element. During those years I rode a 90cc Honda motorcycle, my lifeline for getting to Weaverham Grange, a hospital for the elderly. I would visit the ladies and gentlemen who had been living locally when they were able to look after themselves.

I also visited Winsford and Northwich Infirmary, and it was wonderful. I crocheted more than 300 knee blankets for these hospitals. Others I have sent to Aberdeen, South Wales and the sick and elderly locally. My grandchildren all had one and use them to this day. I made lovely double blankets and use them myself. I sent my woollen blankets to Oxfam and now use the pretty coloured ones, and I can honestly say that I'm sure I got rid of the arthritis in my hands with the exercise of using the needle to make all these.

I was forced to give up my welfare job when I became 80 years old. My health wasn't too good and it meant giving up my motorcycle, but I am still able to visit the sick locally and cheer them up. I find these visits also help me: I get a great deal of satisfaction from it. I have lost at least three of these dear friends in recent months – Mrs Priestner, Mr L Kettle and recently Mr S Forster. The two widows are very dear to me and as long as I can, I shall still visit and help.

Ralph hasn't been well, and this last year or two has cut

Me with my dear grandchildren

down on driving. We only go out locally for pensions and shopping. The family come for us to go visiting or anything special and he is not able to walk much now. Never mind, we must accept these things at our age, for we are very lucky we have each other.

After a very bad time during 1996-97, I was told that I had chronic leukaemia of the lymph glands and that there was no cure. At the same time I needed a pill for my heart every day. When I was told all this it was very blunt and the news didn't seem to sink in. My family doctor did ask me if I had discussed it with any of my family and if I had made any plans, and my answer to that was: "I've had a good think about all this and have decided to think no more about it. I've no intentions of sitting back and wallowing, I've far too much to do and other than my forced visits to Chester to see the specialist, I shall forget all about it."

Here I am still going strong two and a half years later. Oh, if only I could pass my temperament to a lot more sick people to face up to and take what comes, it would help them so much.

After a chance remark to a friend of mine about my childhood, she said: "You should write all that down."

She mentioned it to a friend of hers who belongs to the local history society and I was roped in to join in some discussions at the Salt Museum. I was then asked to give talks at different places and I am really delighted that it has given me a new interest in my life. I am even booked for talks in January and February 2000 and I look forward to that pleasure. Yes, I'll still be here, God willing.

I must tell you of two incidents after Olive's visit. It was our fourth daughter, Tanya's silver wedding and the family had all been invited, but owing to different reasons only myself, Veronica and her husband Clive were able to go. The three of us arrived at the hall and were met by Tanya and John. We got a wonderful reception and I was handed a beautiful bouquet.

I said: "Thank you very much, my dear, but it is your silver wedding and you both are the receivers today."

"Ah," John said, "this has been planned for you for a long time, and I said that if we made twenty five years we would show our thanks to you for all you have done for Tanya."

We all had champagne to celebrate. We had just settled at our table when Tanya brought a lady and gentleman and introduced us to them. They were friends to whom she had told her sad story. The lady said: "I've waited a long time to meet you. May I give you a big hug and join in with all the thanks to you for the love and kindness you gave to Tanya all that time ago when she was in need. Tanya has told me everything and all that happened."

I was so choked I could hardly speak, but did manage to say: "I'm so sorry that Ralph and Diana are not here, because it was their help and understanding that enabled me to cope."

I hadn't realised the effect it had had on that young child. I looked at her, at John and their two beautiful daughters, and felt fit to burst with pride. What a lovely silver lining to what had been a very black cloud.

Since then we have had the first long-term child Sharon to stay for a week. She wanted to come and see her 'Mum and Dad'. She lives in another county and we had not seen her for a number of years.

She wanted to explore the village and to see the changes that had taken place, also to visit the remaining people she knew. One day she went to a garden party for the local nursing home and when she returned she said: "Close your eyes, Mother."

I did so and she said: "Hold out your hands", and a plastic bag was placed on them.

"Now you can open your eyes and see what I've brought you."

Opening the small parcel I found three small ornaments. A white cat, a white armchair with a kitten in it, and a swan with a spray of flowers on one wing. These were all made of white china and tinged with gold leaf, and to me they are worth their weight in gold. Her words as she gave them to me were: "I've got those for you to say 'thank you' for all you have done for me."

How can you begin to explain your feelings at such a sweet gesture? I can't find the words.

She stayed a week and Diana and I saw her on to the train at Crewe. She has rung me up each week to give me orders to take care of myself. Bless her.

*

During the War years the government decided it was time to have children evacuated from the large cities. A lot came to our village Davenham, and one of the billets was Davenham Hall. A couple of rooms were made into dormitories and the children attended the local school. Amongst them were a sister and brother, Virginia, aged four years and Kenneth Osborne, aged seven (no relation to us). They always crossed the road by the hall gates. I think I'm right in saying that on August 1, 1944 Virginia was killed by a van as she crossed over, and nine months afterwards on May 17, 1945 Kenneth was also killed in the same place. The Miss Allens from the Hall had them buried in Davenham church yard. There is an Aberdeen granite headstone and kerb to mark their grave. It was always tended while the Allens were living and I visit their resting place whenever I go there.

I often wonder if somewhere there is a surviving relative, or if they were all killed during the bombing. I don't know whether it was Liverpool or Manchester the evacuees came from, but they came here to be safe and I believe that they were unlucky victims of war.

I told our new vicar about them and asked if he would kindly remember them in his prayers at church. I have also arranged for them to be remembered on November 11 each year with a little wooden cross, because I don't suppose there are many that recall this terrible tragedy.

God bless them, they were someone's children and must not be forgotten.

*

I feel that all this is a fitting end to the simple story of four generations from 1850 to 1999 and I hope, well, I know, that it will be told to my future descendants.

My beloved grandchildren Anthony, Martin, Paul, Sarah and Lindsay begged me to tell my story a long time ago, and at last I have granted them their wish. I do know how pleased they will be, and to my friends who have given me all the encouragement to get it finished I say 'thank you', and to Sandra who triggered it off.

Overleaf you will find quite a number of girls and boys who passed through Davenham School when I was there. I may not have all the names but I have remembered these.

Also there is a list of families and shops – just the village as it was in my young days.

Pupils at Davenham School in 1925

Back row: Walter Thomson, Eric Pattern, Frank Minshall, Jim Ashton, Jack Hayes, Noel Pickering, George Smith.

Third row: Edna Burgess, Freda Breeze, Peggy Buckley, Dorothy Hughes, Evelyn Yarwood, me, Louie Crimes, Marjory Mears, Doris Percival, May Darlington.

Second row: Margaret Robinson, Hilda Minshall, Doreen Evans, Beatty Dean, Joan Platt, Nancy Jack, Daisy Mears, May Stott, Patty Atherton; Mr Harry Smith, head teacher.

Front row: Harold Brownbill, Eddie Lawley, Noel Dutton, Alec Burton, George Rathbone, Keith Ritson, Raymond Phipps.

Pupils' names remembered
1919 — 1928

Girls

Belle Bennet and two sisters
Edith, Lizzie and Pattie Atherton —
    sisters
Maggie, Mabel, Lucy and Hilda Carter
    — sisters
Elsie and Mildred Parry — sisters
Lizzie and Belle Parry — sisters
Evelyn Yarwood (also a sister who died
    in her teens)
Eileen Sherwin
Edith Percival
Doreen Evans
Beatty Dean, Annie Birkett Hogg and
    Jessie Dean — sisters
Flo Byrom
Phylis Tomlinson
Claris Darlington
Linda and May Darlington — sisters
    (different family)
Doris and Nancy Percival — sisters
Maggie Doughty
Minnie and Elsie Jackson — sisters
Rosie Burton and Lena Shaw — step
    sisters
Joyce Foster, Winnie, Molly and Dorothy
    Booth — step sisters
Gladys, Gwen and Hilda Rathbone —
    sisters
Phylis Wright
Phylis and Joan Platt — sisters
Winnie Johnson
Ethel Hickson
Mary Pratt

Dylis Rose
Lily Whittaker
Eva Dartington
Dorothy and Joyce Thornley — sisters
Bertha, Marjorie and Mary Mears —
    sisters
Daisy, Nancy and May Mears — sisters
    (also cousins to above)
Peggy Field
Lucy Millington
Hilda, Ethel, Annie and Kath Tompson
    — sisters
Nellie Dutton
Ethel Towers
Cathleen Moore
Clara and May Pummel — sisters
Edna and Flossie Mills — sisters
Alice and Elsie Hartley — sisters
Freda Dutton
Agnes Rayner
Renee Barlow
Dorothy and Elsie Platt — sisters (and a
    third sister?)
Mona and Renee Wych — sisters
Hilda Minshall
Madge and Vera Shallcross — sisters
Mary and Pegg Dutton — sisters
Nellie, Nancy and May — Tickle sisters
Freda, Connie and Nellie Breeze —
    sisters
Marjorie and Nancy Swindells —
    cousins
Nancy and Louie Gough — sisters
Kittie and Nancy Johnson — sisters

Joyce Brown – bank manager's daughter
Lilly Garner
Marjory Taylor
Freda, Phylis and Rhona Mort – sisters
Edith Parker
Joyce, Annie and Cissie Sharpes – sisters
Molly Hill
Dora Meradith – later married Mr Dean the teacher
Annie, Louie and Clara Crimes – sisters
Betty and Brenda Cross – cousins
Nellie Stringer
Annie, Alma, Ethel, Lucy and Irene Dunn – sisters
Barbara Eyres
Betty Hormbrey
Kathleen and Vivien Tickle – sisters
Edie Shaw
Nellie Oram
Ivy, Annie and Nancy Massey – sisters
Marjorie and Sylvia Smith – sisters
Kathleen Plant
Dylis Phipps
Amy and Evelyn Ashton – sisters
Margaret and Mary Wrench – sisters
Bunty, Bertha and Peggy Minshull – sisters
Peggy Buckley and two sisters
May Stott and sister
Edna and Gladys Burgess – sisters
Joyce and Nellie Whalley – my sister and I
Annie and Edna Brown – sisters
Molly Wright
Margaret Robinson
Alice Rance
Queeny and Ruby Hubble – sisters
Lily Garner

Boys
Jim Ashton
Paul Swindells
Ronnie Wrench
Charlie and Arthur Leach – brothers
Reggie Worth
Bill Arnold
Jeff and Wilf Darlington – brothers
Tommy Buckley and two brothers
Tom Stott
Ossy Whitby
Tom Whitby
Vivian Raynor
Tommy Dutton
George Oram
Eric Lawley
Jimmy Edge
Joey Bray
Roy Clayton
? Birtwistle
Arthur, Joe, Owen, Ronnie and Albert Gough – brothers
Archie Eyres
Sidney Baker
Denis, Basil, Fred and Tom Whyche – brothers
Frank and Alec Minshall – brothers
Noel Pickering
Eric Hughes
Walter and John Tompson – brothers
George Smith
Tom Parry
Noel and Leslie Dutton – brothers
Colin Gowan
Trafford and Jocelyn Sherwin – brothers
Sidney and Sam Johnson – brothers
Doug Stringer
Raymond and Gordon Hind – brothers
George Swindells
Alec and Edgar Taylor – brothers

*An atmospheric photograph of pupils working hard in a classroom
at the old Davenham School*

Robert and John Parker – brothers
Four Sharpes boys
George and Sam Gandy – brothers
Albert Darlington
Stanley, Fred and Oswald Hughes –
    brothers
Quintin and Keith Ritson – brothers
Billy and Joey Field – brothers
Albert Evans
Sam and Tom Moore
Three Hassall Boys
Two Meredith Boys – one drowned in
    the River Weaver
Three Rathbone Boys
Eric Allmark
Bert, Johnny and Robert Crimes –
    brothers
Noel Wright (and brother?)

Harry Stringer
Joe, Johnny and Jimmy Dunn – brothers
Cyril and Les Mort – brothers
Derek Eyres
Len, Sydney and Alf Shaw – brothers
Jack and Frank Butterworth – brothers
Frank Threadgold
Two Massey Boys
Rupert Smith
Bill Brown
Harry Brown
Two Pogson Boys
Walter Swan
Ronnie Moore
Two Hayes Boys
Raymond Phipps
Roy Clayton

The Village

Davenham village as I remember it when I was young:

PEOPLE
The Gentry:
Davenham Hall, Russell Allen, three girls, two boys.
Grove Mount, Stainer Huchins, one girl, one boy. Family
  moved to Whitehall, Hartford and when Mr Stainer
  Hutchins passed away they moved back to Grove Mount.
Davenham House, Malcolms, two sons, not sure of others.
Davenham Lodge, Major Denton, two girls, two boys.
The Church Rectory, Rev George Sandars, five sons, Ted,
  Tim, Tom, Bob and Jim.
Curate's House, standing back by the church. **Next door**
  the bank manager, Mr Brown, one girl
Mrs Braddon, Widow, no children. House now Quincey's.
Whatcroft Hall, Baerlines, two girls, two boys
Bostock Hall, Captain France Hayhurst, widower, one
  daughter.
Mapletops, Dr Doonan, two daughters?

**There was also a number of families with one maid – 5/-
per week jobs.**

BUSINESSES
Bake Houses selling bread or cakes – Platts, Percivals,
  Booths, Mills.
General Store – Gert Davies
General Store and vendor of all china goods and cleaning
  materials – Mrs Buckley
Groceries – Bancrofts, now 913, Goughs, Platts, Percivals.
  Co-op, Mills, later Shouts.
Banks – two.
Post Office – Robinsons.

Davenham centre as it used to be

Paper Shop – Moores, then Harrisons. Now Moores again.

Shoe Shop – Mr Griffiths, now Cutting Crew.

Shaw's Dairy – later Bert Price's store.

Chip Shops – Mrs Perry, Mrs Taylor.

Smithy – Pickerings.

Paraffin oil, wallpaper, paint, etc. – Mrs Mottershaw.

Painter and Decorator – Darlingtons. Stamford Whiteheads paint shop, also decorators.

Haberdashery – Mrs Buckley.

Toffee Shops – Whiteheads and Mrs Barlows. (I own the scales from Whiteheads on which my toffees were weighed 80 and more years ago).

Secondhand Furniture – Mrs Perry.

Butchers – Hardmans, Arnolds.

Public Houses – Bulls Head, Odd Fellows Arms, Platts and Pummells

Jeweller and Watchmaker – Sam Gregory

Doctor Terry's Surgery – 1st house right hand side of Church Street.

Green Grocer – Jimmy Dale, with a horse drawn cart. The horse knew the regular stop at the Public House. Crimes Green Grocer.

Many years ago I believe there was a **dress shop** at 1 Laburnams Lane.

Garages – Stevens, and Whiteheads who were also a taxi service. Also Bonds taxis.

Local old Remedies dating back to 1911

Cold Remedy
1 tablespoon each of glycerine, honey and rum
The juice of 1 large lemon
The yolk of 1 egg

Blend together and put into a jar or wide necked bottle.
Shake well before use.
Dose:- 1 teaspoonful night and morning.

Fruit Salts For Spring
1/2lb icing sugar
2ozs sodium bicarbonate
2ozs tartaric acid
2ozs cream of tartar
2ozs epsom salts
1/2oz magnesia

Roll salts and mix with sugar. Add remainder of ingredients,
magnesia last. Mix well and put in an airtight bottle.
Dose:- 1 teaspoonful every morning.

Headlice
'Precipate' ointment was used in my young days. I don't know
how it was spelt but that's what it sounded like.
It was rubbed into the scalp, left overnight and washed out
the next day, usually Saturday.

Letter from Major Denton to Captain France Hayhurst asking if Mrs Robinson could stay on in her tied cottage at Shipbrook after the death of her husband. He refused.

Index

INDEX

INDEX

Léonie Press specialises in local history and autobiography

MEMORIES OF A CHESHIRE CHILDHOOD – MEMORIAL EDITION
Lenna Bickerton (ISBN 1 901253 00 7)
Lenna describes life in Northwich around the First World War through the sharp senses of a child. Her memories are vivid: duck eggs for breakfast, dancing to Grandad's gramophone, a near tragedy at a watermill, her schooldays, the sights and sounds of the old town, the smells of wild flowers, busy boat traffic on the canal — and the menacing "Ginny Greenteeth." Lenna died in November 1999 and this memorial edition includes her obituary. **£4.99**

A HOUSE WITH SPIRIT
A Dedication to Marbury Hall
Jackie Hamlett and Christine Hamlett (ISBN 1 901253 01 5)
The authors spent three years researching the history of Marbury Hall near Northwich and tracing the lives of its aristocratic and often high-spirited owners. As clairvoyants they have their own theories about its famous ghosts, the Marbury Lady and the Marbury Dunne. They have tapped into the memories they believe still hang around the site of the demolished hall which have enabled them to communicate with its essence. **£8.99**

A NUN'S GRAVE
A novel set in the Vale Royal of England
Alan K Leicester (ISBN 1 901253 08 2)
The Nun's Grave at Vale Royal Abbey has been a source of mystery and ghostly stories for generations of Mid-Cheshire folk. Alan K Leicester's frightening experience there as a young man led him to undertake years of research into the subject and he has woven his findings into a thought-provoking novel on two time-scales. The 14C fates of novice nun Ida Godman and young monk John of Dutton become inextricably entwined with the present-day lives of newly-weds Ian and Jane who buy a house on the site of the abbey. The author stresses that his enthralling book is fiction and not scholarship. **£7.99**

110

DIESEL TAFF
From 'The Barracks' to Tripoli
Austin Hughes (ISBN 1 901253 14 7)

Austin Hughes was born in February 1922 at 'The Barracks', a group of flea-ridden cottages deep in rural North Wales. His book tells how he grew up as an abstemious god-fearing country lad, innocent of the world outside. From childhood he had loved heavy machinery and he learned to drive trucks and bulldozers. Then in 1940 he was called up to join the Royal Engineers. This was to be an experience which changed the young Welshman's life and earned him his nick-name 'Diesel Taff'. By the end of the war, he'd been to 18 countries, travelling thousands of miles across deserts and mountains, transporting heavy plant, building roads and air strips, clearing avalanches and ferrying refugees. The book gives fascinating insights into life in pre-war rural Wales as well as describing the daily experiences and duties of an R.E. sapper driver in WW2.
Available at the end of April 2000: £8.99

THE WAY WE WERE
Omnibus edition incorporating Over My Shoulder and Another's War
Les Cooper (ISBN 1 901253 07 4)

This book is an omnibus edition of Les Cooper's Crewe memories "Over My Shoulder" and "Another's War", originally published separately in 1996 by Crewe and Nantwich Borough Council when the author was mayor, and now reprinted by popular demand.
The first work describes his childhood in the railway town during the Depression and the second his war experiences as an apprentice in a reserved occupation at the LMS Railway Works. **£7.99**

AVAILABLE FROM THE END OF JUNE 2000:
WOOLLYBACK by ALAN FLEET

This moving and evocative novel is set in Winsford, Cheshire and studies the prejudice between the inhabitants of Over and Wharton in one generation and between the Liverpudlian overspill 'Scousers' and the native 'Woollybacks' in the next, through the eyes of a father and son. **£8.99**

**All these books can be ordered from The Léonie Press,
13 Vale Road, Hartford, Northwich, Cheshire CW8 1PL
Tel 01606 75660 Fax: 01606 77609 e-mail: anne@aloaderpubs.u-net.com
For the latest information visit our website: www.leoniepress.co.uk**

111